PSYCHOLOGICAL FACTORS
IN
COMPETITIVE SPORT

PSYCHOLOGICAL FACTORS IN COMPETITIVE SPORT

by
Don Davies

with
Malcolm Armstrong

 The Falmer Press

(A member of the Taylor & Francis Group)
London ● New York ● Philadelphia

UK   The Falmer Press, Falmer House, Barcombe, Lewes,
East Sussex BN8 5DL

USA   The Falmer Press, Taylor & Francis Inc., 242 Cherry Street,
Philadelphia, PA 19106–1906

First published 1989

British Library Cataloguing in Publication Data
Davies, Don
   Psychological factors in competitive sport.
   1. Sports. Psychological aspects
   I. Title
   796'.01
   ISBN 1-85000-606-7
   ISBN 1-85000-607-5 pbk

Library of Congress Cataloging-in-Publication Data
Davies, Don, 1928-
   Psychological factors in competitive sport / by Don Davies.
      p.   cm.
   Bibliography: p.
   Includes index.
   ISBN 1-85000-606-7. – ISBN 1-85000-607-5 (pbk.)
   1. Sports – Pyschological aspects.
   2. Sports – Study and teaching.
   3. Coaching (Athletics) – Psychological aspects.
   I. Title.
GV706.4.D38   1989
796'.01 – dc20

Jacket design by Caroline Archer

*Typeset in 10½/13 Bembo by
The FD Group Ltd, Fleet, Hampshire*

*Printed in Great Britain by Taylor & Francis (Printers) Ltd,
Basingstoke*

Contents

Preface

The psychology of sport is an applied psychology. It is the science of psychology applied to sport and attempts to describe, explain and predict achievement and performance in sport. Sports psychology embraces such fundamental concerns and concepts as motivation, arousal levels, skill acquisition, feedback, reinforcement, anticipation, psychological preparation, attention, attitudes, emotional health and the management of stress. Several of these concerns have been the subject of extensive scientific investigation for a number of decades. As a result, it is possible to suggest guidelines based upon sound, well established psychological principles for the realization of athletic potential.

Historically, the coaching of athletes has largely emphasized the development of technical ability and physical fitness to the neglect of critical psychological factors. Psychological principles have been followed, but in a haphazard rather 'ad hoc' way. This in part is a reflection of tradition. Although it is widely appreciated that mental and emotional states can make the difference between winning and losing, the role of psychology in sport has largely been restricted to pre-match advice and instruction. This is likely to be of little value. Indeed for players who are already highly activated or 'psyched up', the rousing pre-match 'pep' talk is almost certain to be counterproductive and result in a deterioration in performance.

The demands of competition are such that the psychological preparation of sportspeople needs to be carried out over a prolonged period of time for it to be effective. Psychological skills, such as self-confidence and concentration, are only required as a result of extensive practice. Telling people to concentrate or to relax, for example, without telling them *how* is quite a meaningless instruction. Thus advising a tennis player as he goes on court to concentrate is akin to telling him to go out and serve for the first time.

Psychological Factors in Competitive Sport deals principally with the development of ability, the maximization of performance in competition, and the emotional health, social adjustment and general well-being of the aspiring champion. Competitive sport is testing and demanding psychologically. Participants should be sufficiently emotionally mature and appropriately trained to cope with stress if they are to gain satisfaction and to derive benefit from the experience.

Terminology

The terms arousal, anxiety, stress and coping are used frequently throughout this book. Though closely related, they are quite separate constructs. A description of all four terms is given in the relative chapters but in the interests of clarity the four terms are defined and described below.

Arousal

This term refers to the degree of the intensity of behaviour. The level of arousal can be regarded as a continuum ranging from deep sleep at the one end through normal resting states to a high degree of high excitement at the other (Duffy, 1957). Arousal can be measured by heart rate, pulse rate, muscle respiration, tension and by skin conductance and the galvanic skin response among other indices. Arousal interacts with anxiety. Although it is commonly believed that heightened anxiety levels will be accompanied by heightened arousal levels this is not always the case. A high level of anxiety, for example, may result in fatigue and an accompanying low level of arousal. Again the presence of an audience, such as an interviewing panel, causes some people to become very anxious but with an accompanying low level of arousal indicated by generally listless responses to questions. And in sport some players under intense pressure freeze and fail to perceive and react to stimuli.

Anxiety

Anxiety is a somewhat diffuse emotional condition which can be maladaptive in its functions. Anxiety can be viewed both as an enduring personality factor or trait, A-trait, and also as a temporary state, A-state, which is evoked by a specific situation. Interactions between A-trait and A-state occur and a high level of trait anxiety generally predisposes individuals to have elevated A-state anxiety levels in situations which are perceived as stressful.

Stress

Stress can be defined as the demands which the environment places on the individual. It can be viewed from the standpoint of testing man in much the same way as testing machines. Because of highly individualistic reactions to stress it is generally more helpful to talk of perceived stress. The degree of stress attached to a situation is dependent to a large extent upon the perceptions of the individual which are the product of his emotional disposition, his previous experiences, his abilities, the need for achievement and the perceived importance of the event amongst other factors. Specific factors external to the individual, such as the presence of an audience and other situational variables operate to influence the stress attached to a particular activity.

Coping

The term coping is used frequently in the literature concerned with stress management and test-anxiety reduction. The term is used to denote all mechanisms employed by a person to meet perceived threats to his prestige and self-esteem. An individual is presumed to be coping in a positive way if his behaviour consists of responses to environmental influences which enable him to master situations.

Introduction

The purpose of this book is to explain the importance of psychological or 'mental' and emotional factors for achievement and performance in competitive sport. The book is based on tried and tested methods in teaching and on extensive research findings in the field of sports psychology. It has two main aims. The first is to select and outline ways by which young people can learn to become highly skilled and well-adjusted sportsmen. The second main aim is to describe the techniques by which young players, having become highly skilled, can do justice to their ability and commitment to the extent that they are able to perform consistently at their peak in the highly stressful sports situation.

The book has a strong practical orientation. Well-established psychological techniques and strategies for achievement in sport are advanced and explained in detail and in some depth. Apart from chapter 7, each chapter refers to specific guidelines to be followed and detailed practices to be undertaken. Chapter 3, in particular, has a substantially practical emphasis and contains a considerable amount of up-to-date information concerning the teaching of skill in sport.

The importance of psychological factors such as confidence, anxiety and concentration is generally well recognized. In tennis, for example, there are players who play very well in practice 'knock ups' but in the competitive match situation become so nervous that their game becomes sprinkled with unforced errors such as double faults and other simple mistakes. On the other hand, there are players who really enjoy the competitive match situation and always seem to play to the best of their ability and to beat players possessing superior technique and skill.

It is also the case that at each recognized level of ability, whether it be junior county level, senior county level or world class level, there is often very little difference between the actual playing abilities of the competitors. It is often the psychological factors which decide the difference between winning and losing. This seems to be the general view among many players at the very top of their sport and it is borne out by such comments as 'It's all in the mind' and 'Confidence is everything'. Former world champion golfer, Arnold Palmer, considers that 'golf is 90 per cent from the shoulders up' and other international players are of the firm belief that the game is played on a six inch course — between the ears!

More sophisticated training methods and increased sponsorship in sport mean that standards are rising all the time and more and more people are reaching the top in their chosen sport. As a result psychological factors are assuming even greater importance than formerly.

Yet despite this situation relatively little has been written concerning the psychological dynamics of sports performance in a competitive context. There are many books which deal with the technical and physical aspects of the game and hundreds of coaches to develop the playing capacities of the players. There are very few books, however, which deal in any depth with the psychological aspects of sport, although it is evident even to the casual onlooker that tournament tennis, for example, particularly at the junior level, is fraught with emotional problems, worries, frustrations and sometimes despair. It is clear that at all levels of competition players can be beset with psychological problems and some obviously have great difficulty in coping. For those trying to make their way in tennis, for example, the pervading philosophy is that 'Winning isn't everything, it's the only thing'. Thus in this context the psychological pressures are immense. In these circumstances only wins count. Wins equate with success and losses with failure. At the qualifying events of the major international events and the national junior championships the stresses are greatest. This is evidenced by the unusually high number of simple mistakes and the negative emotional and behavioural reactions of many of the players. Talented young players who are not psychologically tough or resilient or who have not been trained to cope with stress frequently fail to go beyond this stage and matches in which they are involved are often lost rather than won.

The emotional health of young people in competitive sport is indeed a neglected area of concern. The emphasis on continual competition, which is the case in several sports, means that by the age of 16 many young sportspeople are emotionally 'burnt out' and abandon their sport altogether. The introduction of competition even as early as 6 in some sports has led a number of National Health Bodies to take a serious look at the wisdom of competitive sport in the very young.

Few stress-prone competitors can expect to receive any effective help or guidance. Thus the majority of young sportspeople are left to muddle through what is unchartered territory in a psychological sense. This is a pity for effective practices are available for the management of stress and consequently the control of concentration. Competitive sport situations frequently exert pressures upon young people which call for much more than ordinary effort. Consequently, the traditional approach concentrating almost exclusively on the physical aspects of sport is too narrowly based and inadequate for the preparatory needs of many aspiring young competitors. What is required is a wider more sustained systematic approach which is concerned with the emotional health and development of the individual. Such an approach is needed not only for the enhancement of performance but also for the general well-being of the young sportsmen.

The idea for the book stems from an ongoing research project conducted by the author into the poor performance of British tennis players (men) at international level. The fact is that with a few isolated exceptions, British men's tennis has been in the doldrums for more than forty years. In the decade since tennis turned professional in 1969, the British record at Wimbledon is one semi-finalist (Roger Taylor) and four players in the last sixteen. Jeremy Bates, ranked number 2 in Britain, reached the third round at Wimbledon in 1987 and was only the second player to do so in five years. Our performance is equally unimpressive with respect to the other major world tennis championships. Not only, however, does Britain fail to produce champions but its representation is generally very 'thin on the ground' at the highest level of international competition. Judging by the ATP world ranking list published in September 1987, there seems to be little prospect of any immediate improvement in the status of the British game. The list shows that Britain's number 1 player, Andrew Castle, was ranked 127.

It is from tennis that the examples and illustrations in the text are largely taken. Tennis is a game which is frequently full of stressful situations. The very nature of the scoring system particularly with respect to the 'deuce' device means that the crowd can be provided with almost continual stress. Added to this there are net-cords, miss-hits, bad bounces, doubtful line decisions, all of which mean that close tennis matches are generally highly charged with tension, typified perhaps, at the extreme, by the atmosphere at the Royal Albert Hall during Wightman Cup matches between Great Britain and the United States. Thus tennis provides a unique opportunity to examine the importance of psychological factors for achievement in sport. The illustrations drawn from tennis have particular significance for other individual competitive games and for a number of other sports in general.

Chapter 1 looks at various motivational strategies and techniques and argues the case for developing intrinsic motivation in young sportspeople. The merits and dangers of competition are examined. Chapters 2 and 3 are largely concerned with the psychological aspects of practice and coaching. Chapter 4 examines at length the relationship between anxiety, stress and performance. Strategies and techniques for the management of competitive stress are set out in considerable detail. Chapter 5 studies the phenomenon of anticipation and demonstrates how this skill in ball games is best acquired. Chapter 6 looks at a recently emerging concept in sport, that of psychological preparation for competition, and chapter 7 continues with a discussion of the importance of psychological factors for performance in sport. The final chapter is devoted to the question of self-confidence in sport. It is based partly on well-established psychological strategies and techniques and partly on the author's own experience of working with young people as they prepare for competition in both sport and for public examinations in the academic field where the pressures can be immense. There are hardly any books which deal with this area in sport in any depth nor in any extensively applied way. Self-confidence virtually dictates success or failure in competitive sport as it does in any stressful test situation. Yet this concern is widely neglected in most sports. The general view is that confidence is something you either have or you don't — that it just happens. This crucial factor in a number of sports is generally at best based on hunches and at worst left to chance. It is emphasized in this chapter that confidence is a quality which can be generated. The aim being that the young sportsperson will be able to do full justice to his ability and commitment. Strategies and techniques for generating confidence are set out and are underpinned by the discussion and evidence cited in previous chapters. They are summarized in chapter 8 for ease of reference and to give the reader an overview of the whole question of confidence for achievement in sport.

Chapter 1

Learning, Motivation and Performance

Introduction

The study of learning and motivation is important because it seems to be fairly certain that the majority of sportsmen in general and tennis players in particular, fail to fulfil their potential ability. The barrier to progress seems to be a psychological one — a classical example being the attempts to break the 4 minute mile in the early 1950s. This psychological barrier is largely determined by a player's own expectations of the standards he will reach. A number of principles and strategies are advanced for motivating young sports people to continue to develop their skill. The importance of an individual approach is emphasized because of the varying needs of particular players who really need to be treated often in quite different ways. Thus, if a coach is to help motivate a player he must really come to know him as a person.

In this chapter the relationship between success and failure and motivation is examined together with how this influences levels of aspiration or of expectancy of future success. The effect of praise and criticism on the motivation of players is also discussed.

The coach's expectation of a player's potential can be a very powerful factor influencing the motivation to continue to practise. With respect to his match and tournament performance an individual will very often fulfil the expectations of his coach, tending to do well if these are high and optimistic and tending to do badly if these expectations are low and pessimistic. There is, in fact, much research ouside sport, particularly in the education field, concerning the powerful influence which the expectations of 'significant others' has on an individual's own motivation and expectations. By 'significant others' is meant the people who are regarded by the player as being important. In tennis this is likely to be the coaches and the selectors of the representative teams and training squads.

Considerable attention is given to the relationship between the intensity of motivation or level of arousal and performance in the competitive match situation. Generally people play best at moderate levels of arousal and there is, in fact, an optimum level of arousal for maximum performance for each player. It is at the two extremes of high and low levels of arousal that individuals do least well.

Individual differences in levels of intensity between people before competitive events mean that to perform at their best some players will need to be 'psyched up' and others to be 'psyched down' to use the American expressions. Care must be taken to see that young competitors do not become over-aroused, excited and agitated resulting inevitably in a deterioration in their performance. As is the practice with the managers of some professional football clubs, for example, exhorting highly aroused players to show still greater effort is counterproductive, bringing some of them to a state of near hysteria. They are effectively 'psyched out' before the game even starts. This is evidenced by the number of goals which are missed when it should have been much easier to have scored.

Ways in which motivation can be enhanced are discussed and the final section of this chapter is concerned with a very serious discussion of the intensity of arousal and performance and the implications for the coach who has a crucial role to play.

Reaching international level in any major sport involves a long, arduous course of practice and training extending over many years. Progress rarely takes a uniform path and the way to the top is characterized by ups and downs in performance interspersed by periods when no improvement or apparent improvement is taking place.

Learning

Progress towards becoming efficient in any athletic activity can be represented graphically by a learning curve. In plotting such a curve or progress chart the horizontal axis measures the number of successive trials or practice sessions and it is usual for the vertical axis to measure performance although sometimes it will measure time or the number of errors. If performance is measured the curve rises with increasing practice; if time or the number of errors is measured the curve falls. A learning curve reveals the rate of improvement and also changes in this rate. As we would expect most curves show variations in the rate of improvement. Curves measuring learning for most sports (Figure 1) are generally negatively accelerating, that is to say they show the fastest rate of gain in the early stages of practice and the slowest rate as an individual approaches the limits of his ability. Such a curve tends to occur when the activity is relatively easy and when people become bored with the sport and begin to lose interest. Sooner or later all learning curves will show a slowing down in the rate of improvement. This is because part of the practice sessions will be spent in merely maintaining the gains already achieved. As learning advances this tends to be true to a progressively greater extent with players having to spend progressively more and more time in practice merely to maintain the level of efficiency already achieved. Then too, as a player begins to approach the limits of his ability it takes more effort and more time to improve still further. Other factors, such as fatigue, a sense of sufficiency, the lack of desire for further advancement and inappropriate practice in the form of the needless repetition of basic skills and routines which have already been thoroughly mastered and which players see as being quite pointless.

The message of this for the aspiring sportsperson is that he cannot expect the same improvement as previously from the same amount of practice. It is important for people to know that this is almost inevitable

Figure 1: Idealized learning curve

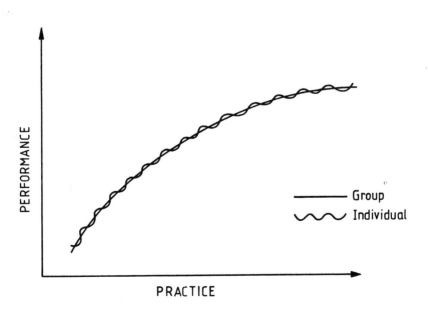

and that younger competitors will be seen to be 'catching up' as they need less practice to improve at their lower level of skill.

Plateaux are a common feature of most learning curves. These are graphically represented by a horizontal stretch in the curve indicating a phase when little or no measured change takes place (Figure 2). Plateaux can appear at various stages in the learning process and generally indicate only a temporary halt to improvement. A plateau in a learning curve does not necessarily mean that learning is not taking place. It may be that various aspects of a player's game, skill or technique are undergoing improvement which are not reflected in overall performance. Once these have been integrated and consolidated the learning curve will rise again. In more simple terms latent or 'hidden' learning could be taking place over the span of the 'plateau' as it is indicated by performance scores.

Figure 2: Idealized learning curve with plateaux

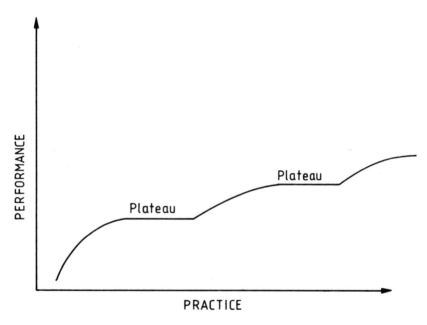

Plateaux can be discouraging for players trying to improve upon their performance, and from the motivational point of view they are best avoided. The coach can be of considerable help at this stage by giving encouragement and support. He/she should point out that everybody is beset with such periods in their development when it seems that the standard of play has become more or less static.

Composite scores for a group of players as they are represented on a graph can provide the coach with valuable information. Apart from indicating the general course of progress any pronounced dip or sudden rise is likely to reflect a potent factor which is common to the group or squad of players. For young sportspeople, as with workers in industry, the graph can be a powerful motivational device in that it presents a graphic, objective description of improvement.

Smooth curves of learning, such as in Figure 1, only occur for large groups of people and result from the averaging out of individual performance scores. For a single individual a learning curve seldom rises smoothly for successive practices. Whilst a general upward trend can frequently be seen, individual learning curves are characterized by a great deal of zigzagging. In the course towards becoming a highly skilled sportsman there are inevitable fluctuations in performance and there are periodic surges and setbacks. Fluctuations in performance occur because of the numerous factors such as motivation, health, concentration among others which serve to influence learning. Some factors facilitate skill acquisition whilst others inhibit improvement. These factors can operate in various ways from one practice session to another and from one match to another. Fluctuations in performance therefore arise because of variations which occur in the factors involved and the way they may interact with each other. On some days a games player for example, feels confident, is seeing the ball and everything is going well for him/her. On other days he/she may not be concentrating so well, his/her attention wanders and he/she becomes anxious and depressed about his/her play. These temporary mood swings occur for most players at some time and their cause is not always easy to ascertain.

Motivation is discussed at length in the following section but the use by the coach of individual learning curves can be of considerable motivational value. They provide graphic, objective and measurable evidence of a player's progress. Any progress which a player makes is there for him/her to see and this information is a powerful incentive to continue his/her efforts in trying to develop his/her ability. Charts of progress also provide the opportunity to use a good motivational technique which is to compete against oneself. That is to say a player can compete against his/her previous performances. Charts are a source of valuable information for they enable the player to relate his/her performance to his/her preparation for that performance. In this way he/she is able, with experience, to select the most effective approach to make. In tennis graphs can be drawn up to indicate progress with the service and other strokes in terms of their accuracy, control and consistency. Graphs of test results from physical fitness measures can also be outlined.

Generally, it is the results of matches which are taken as being the measure of a player's progress. This can be a very inaccurate yardstick and there are several reasons for this fallibility. In many cases the margin between a win and a loss can be very close indeed as is evidenced by matches which are won on the tie-break in tennis. Again parts of a player's game may be undergoing improvement but this improvement has still to be reflected in match and tournament performance in terms of results. Further tennis players, for example, can be winning at junior level with the sort of game which will certainly not succeed at senior international level which has been a characteristic of the game in this country for decades. Players who take a long-term view and go for big powerful strokes and a generally ambitious game may lose out at junior level but if they have the courage of their convictions, with increasing mastery they will do best in the end. Through lack of early success, however, they may become despondent and give up. Charts which provide valid measures of progress in terms of skilled performance measures should encourage them to continue.

Motivation

Motivation can be defined as being aroused to action, to directed purposeful behaviour although this may not necessarily be either efficient or effective. The study of motivation is important because it seems fairly certain that with the exception of the few champions in sport the majority of young players seldom fulfil their potential. Given the opportunity most young players could do much better. This is true for all sports and not just tennis and arises in the main from motivational problems.

In sportsmen as in other spheres of skill acquisition improvements in performance tend to decrease as the limits of ability are approached. This is partly due to the fact that there is a slowing down in the rate at which people are able to continue to improve. At moderate levels of ability progress can readily be seen and is sometimes quite marked. At the higher levels of performance, however, much of the time spent in practice will be spent solely in maintaining these levels. As players continue to improve this tends to be true to a progressively greater extent with more and more of a player's practice time being spent in maintaining standards. Thus at relatively high levels of play it takes more effort, more time to improve further and it becomes increasingly difficult to make progress. Indeed once champion players drop out of any sport for any length of time the old adage: 'They never come back' holds true for most. In so many cases a return to the game is at a lower standard than formerly.

For the aspiring player the problem sooner or later becomes largely one of motivation. In many cases there is the belief that further improvement is simply not possible. If a player now perceives that this is also the belief of the coach then it is highly likely that these expectations of his limits will be confirmed. As we have noted earlier, the coach's expectation of performance is a powerful factor determining perform-ance levels and has led to much research outside sport concerning the so-called self-fulfilling prophecy. Generally a person's performance tends to confirm the expectations of 'significant others' or those who are perceived as having some credibility. Thus an optimistic approach by a coach or teacher tends to arouse higher motivational levels and expectations in the player and a pessimistic approach to result in a lowering of motivational levels and of expectations.

Many players experience periods when they become convinced that they have reached the limits of performance and that further improve-ment is simply not possible. An optimistic, insightful and supportive coach has a crucial role to play in encouraging the player to persist at such times and to tackle difficulties in a positive way. Players can be helped if it is pointed out that temporary halts to progress are not uncommon in the acquisition of skill in sports. The coach can point out that latent learning can be taking place which is not immediately reflected in performance measures.

Intrinsic and extrinsic motivation and a combination of these two are the only forms which motivation can take. Extrinsically motivated people are engaging in a particular activity or sport for the rewards which go with success. They are playing for the status of being in a team or squad or they are playing for the medals, cups or the financial rewards which can be obtained. On the other hand, when a person is intrinsically motivated he/she is engaging in the sport for its own sake, for the satisfaction, for the sheer enjoyment that it brings. Many of the top players in sport get tremendous satisfaction from having complete mastery over a skill and being able to perform it in expert fashion. They are not satisfied with moderate standards and go to great lengths to become perfectionists for the personal satisfaction which this brings. They enjoy the challenge of the pursuit of excellence. Intrinsic motivation is generally associated with greater persistence and greater commitment. For people who are essentially extrinsically motivated to play sport that is, they are concerned mainly with the rewards which accompany achievement, then if the rewards become difficult to achieve or unobtainable they may well lose interest. The real danger also exists that where people are encouraged to play by being offered rewards they may sense that they are being manipulated, that other people are controlling their behaviour. It does happen that people who were initially intrinsically motivated lose this interest on being offered rewards and prizes. On the other hand a reward could be perceived by a person as increasing the importance of a particular achievement so that it becomes more prestigious than formerly. With greater feelings of personal competence intrinsic motivation is likely to be enhanced.

The following example illustrates how the introduction of rewards can cause a change from intrinsically to extrinsically motivated behaviour.

> An old man lived alone on a street where boys played noisily every afternoon. One day the din became too much, and he called the boys into his house. He told them he liked to listen to them play, but his hearing was failing and he could no longer hear their games. He asked them to come around each day and play noisily in front of his house. If they did, he would give them each a quarter. The youngsters raced back the following day and made a tremendous racket in front of the house. The old man paid them, and asked them to return the next day. Again they made noise, and again the old man paid them for it. But this time he gave each boy only 20 cents, explaining that he was running out of money. On the following day, they got only 15 cents each. Furthermore, the old man told them, he would have to reduce the fee to five cents on the fourth day. The boys became angry, and told the old man they would not be back. It was not worth the effort, they said, to make a noise for only five cents a day.
>
> (Casady, 1974)

Contrary to popular belief young players place great importance on being really good at a sport and not just on winning. It is important, therefore, that situations are created which give the young player the opportunity to develop his ability to pursue excellence. In the section which follows strategies for enhancing the intrinsic motivation of players are outlined.

How to Motivate Young Sports People

Several well-established motivational strategies can be employed to encourage young people to persist with their practice and training over extended periods of time. People differ markedly in their personalities, abilities and past experiences to the extent that they just cannot be treated all in the same way. Differences in personality, for example, mean that harsh criticism might be accepted by a tough-minded individual but at the same time could be a devastating, demoralizing experience for a relatively, sensitive young person. It is imperative therefore that motivational strategies be individually focused. This means, as Cratty (1973) has pointed out, that if a coach is to be effective he must really get to know the player as a person. In this regard it helps to meet, observe and work with the young player in a variety of situations. Weekly discussions or chats of personal concerns on an individual basis in a relaxed, informal atmosphere can be a great help and often serve to prevent problems such as a negative attitude from developing. It is of fundamental importance therefore that the coach learns to recognize differences between players not only with respect to physical maturity and ability but also in terms of emotional maturity and sensitivity if he is to be a successful motivator. Each young sportsperson is unique.

Motivational Strategies

The aspiring championship player needs to be continuously motivated. As a first step, specific, realistic goals or objectives need to be planned. Goals need to be set which are not too easy, not too difficult yet at the same time are interesting and set a challenge. This means that goals set for players will vary according to their individual needs. The overriding consideration is for training, practice and playing sessions to be both meaningful and enjoyable. Goals should be discussed with the players. Participation in planning generally means that the player becomes more involved in the programme and more committed because he/she feels responsible to some extent concerning what he/she has to to. The mutual planning of goals means that young players feel that their actions are self-determined and provide a sense of personal compe-tence. As a consequence intrinsic motivation is likely to be enhanced.

Young players need to have a lot of success. Knapp (1964) has argued that the initial experience of any sports activity may influence an individual's attitude towards it for a long time. Certainly early experiences of failure generally mean people soon lose interest and enthusiasm for an activity. Thus upsetting experiences must be avoided and first impressions of a game should be both meaningful and enjoyable. Early experiences are closely related to the level of aspiration or the expectancy of success. Generally failure experiences lead to a fall in aspiration levels with people expecting to do less well. Success on the other tends to lead to an increase in aspiration levels with people now expecting to improve on their current performance. What is well-recognized is that aspiration levels or the expectancy of success or failure determine to a very large extent the level of *actual* performance. Thus it is invariably the case that if people expect to succeed then they succeed and if they expect to fail then they fail. We have said that it is important in the early stages of playing a game for young players to experience, in their view, a considerable amount of success. However, successes and failures do not necessarily equate with wins and losses, for much depends on the perceived difficulty of the contest. A player, for example, could very well see an actual loss as a success if he put up a performance which was above his expectations. At the same time a 'win' over a much inferior player might hardly count as a success and indeed is likely to be totally ignored.

For the fairly well-established player who has already made some progress in the game and is moderately skilful then the best results seem to come from a mixture of failure and success. The danger with a period of long continued success is that it can lead to boredom, disinterest and complacency. Playing the game no longer presents much of a challenge and there is little excitement for the player. Certainly it seems to be the case that occasional failure for the maturing player can act as an incentive to try harder and in this way can be highly motivating.

The causes of success and failure which individuals attribute to competitive situations in sport seem likely to influence motivation and thus subsequent achievement. Causal attributions have been found to include ability, effort, luck and difficulty of task (Weiner *et al.* 1971). Work by Spink (1978) showed that competitors attributed success and failure to certain stable factors, particularly ability. Consistently successful people, for example, attributed this to their high ability whereas people who were consistently unsuccessful attributed this to their low ability. This finding suggests that people with high ability are likely to try for even higher performance levels. On the other hand, consistent failure may well lead people to believe that they have little ability for a sport. As a consequence, they make little effort and may withdraw from the activity altogether.

Praise and Criticism

There are often marked variations in the reactions of people to praise and criticism. These variations can occur as the result of personality factors and differences in the rates of progress among individual players. To be effective any praise or criticism which may be used by the coach must be closely related to the varying needs of individual players. The effect of any praise or criticism will be strongly influenced by a young player's opinion of his coach. The coach who is held in high regard is likely to have a considerable influence on young players. On the other hand the coach who is held in low regard is hardly likely to influence young people to any extent since he is perceived as having little credibility.

Praise must be warranted. Too much praise especially if it is not warranted is likely to have little effect and can be counter-productive. Use of praise can be irritating in the case of a player who clearly sees that he/she is not improving. Thus the use of praise must be deserved and must be seen to be deserved. Praise must be contiguous. It should be given during or immediately following the completion of the activity, say a tournament match, and it can be given for such various things as effort, particular strokes, speed of movement and tactical skill, apart from the result. In general, warranted praise is a powerful motivating strategy encouraging the young player to persist with his/her training, practice and playing schedule.

In general people who are making progress in the sport seem to benefit most from a mixture of praise and criticism. A combination of praise and criticism is generally more effective than praise used alone and criticism used alone. However, it must be repeated that a highly individual approach is important because of the marked variations in people's reactions to praise and criticism. Thus the coach must seek to relate to a person in terms of his/her sensitivity and progress and standing in the game. What is required and what is appreciated by young people is constructive criticism which is concerned with specific technical suggestions for improvement both in terms of skill and attitude. Exhortations to try harder, to concentrate more will be meaningless in the absence of being instructed *how* to do these things.

Individual Coaching and Recognition

It is of paramount importance that coaching is individually focused. Players need to have regular individual attention and to feel that their accomplishments are being recognized. Experiments conducted at the Hawthorne Works of the Western Electric Company at their plant in Chicago, USA, from 1926 to 1939 demonstrated the importance of taking an individual interest in people. The working conditions at the site were manipulated in various ways. These included better heating and lighting and longer and more frequent rest and refreshment periods. Production rose. However when these working conditions were made less favourable production still continued to rise. No tangible reason for increased production could be identified. Eventually the researchers were forced to the conclusion that increased production was the result not of any single change in the working conditions but because of the special interest which was being taken in the members of the workforce as *people*. The feeling grew among the workers that they were no longer being treated as mere cogs in an industrial machine. This special interest resulted in increased morale and greater commitment on the part of the workers. Numerous subsequent studies have demonstrated the importance in teaching and coaching of a highly individualized approach and the need to get to know the young person. Botterill (1980) argues strongly that the coach should be not only concerned with athletic progress, but should be involved with a player's personal growth and development. Successful international athletes, Botterill maintains, are generally those who have stable personalities and whose personal growth and development have not been neglected. The concern of the total development of the young person is frequently a necessary prerequisite for the pursuit of excellence in sport.

Good Teaching

Well-organized, well-planned practice sessions with clearly established, attainable objectives are highly motivating. They need to be conducted with enthusiasm and with plenty of verbal encouragement. Practice sessions need to be very active with all the participants being almost continually engaged. Talks and discussions should be kept to the minimum.

Competition

Used wisely competition can be a valuable motivational technique. Competition must be closely related to the needs of individual players. Practice drills such as hitting targets, maintaining rallies, racing for short balls, can be made competitive and the novelty and fun of these often enhances motivation. However, there are dangers which are implicit in competitive situations. Some competitive situations, for example, can generate high levels of stress resulting in a feeling of anxiety and emotional tension, particularly when seemingly great importance is attached to the results. Motivation will be weakened if an individual is continually winning with great ease. Likewise, motivation will be weakened if an individual is being continually outclassed. This will be particularly so if deficiencies are publicly exposed in the presence of a critical audience. This latter situation poses a real threat to a young person's self-esteem and emotional health and can generate negative attitudes concerning the sport.

The value of competition varies according to the ability of the players. Competition, for example, between low skilled players tends to disrupt performance and thus to have an adverse effect on progress. On the other hand, competition between highly skilled players tends to enhance performance and thus to facilitate further progress. Competition must be used with the needs of the players being kept carefully in mind. Competition should be used to provide enjoyment and to give a gradually increasing edge and sharpness to the practice.

Knapp (1964) is firmly of the belief that unless competitive situations are carefully handled there can be a real risk of antagonisms arising both between individuals and between groups. Knapp also argues that competition can impede progress when young players concentrate too much on winning at a particular level and in tennis, for example, rely largely on a safe, defensive game and neglect to develop the stroke repertoire needed to succeed at international level.

Competition against the self is an excellent motivational strategy which avoids the tensions and antagonisms which can occur when people compete against each other. The value of competition is considerable when an individual is competing against him/herself in the sense that he/she is trying to improve on his/her own previous level of performance or score. Intra-competition presents a meaningful challenge and provides the opportunity to analyze performance in an objective way free from the subjective bias which arises in some inter-competitive situations. A player can also compete against recognized, established standards of performance which pertain in particular sports. Apart from its motivational value, intra-competition provides the performer with informational feedback. The coach therefore should be creating practice situations which provide the individual players with objective knowledge of the results of his performance. Knowledge of the results of performance in tennis, for example, can come in the form of hitting targets, in the length and accuracy of rallies in various forms and, in the case of the service, with the speed or power of the shot. With a little ingenuity a good enough estimate can be obtained without the use of a timing machine.

Motivation and Performance

Motivation has been discussed so far with regard to improving levels of skill and of playing ability in terms of commitment and of practice. The following section is concerned with the intensity of motivation in terms of arousal or of activation of the nervous system and how this influences performance in a competitive match context. Some psychological aspects of sports performance are discussed at length and in some depth. Guidelines which help players to be at their best mentally for a match or tournament are outlined. Because of the widely differing needs of individual players, the importance of an individual approach is underlined. Players just cannot all be helped in the same way. Some anxious players, for example, can be 'psyched up' before a contest to the extent that they are effectively 'psyched out' and fail to do justice to their talents in a competitive match. The coach's knowledge of a player in terms of his temperament, ability and current tournament perform-ance is an important factor in planning the appropriate motivational strategy. Players must be 'known' by their coaches in these respects if they are to be helped to be at their best mentally and emotionally.

The intensity of motivation is a crucial factor in competitive sports performance and is closely concerned with levels of arousal in the individual. Arousal refers to the degree of activation of the nervous system and can be regarded as a continuum of activity which ranges from deep sleep at the one end through normal waking states to one of extreme alertness and high excitement at the other. Arousal levels can be measured although some difficulty exists here when comparing groups because the physiological reactions of people to stress in the form of heart rate, blood pressure and sweating, for example, tend to be highly individualistic.

When an individual becomes emotionally aroused there is generally an increase in perspiration. This means that the resistance of the skin to the passage of an electric current is lowered. Thus conductive levels will be high when the individual is highly motivated and will be low when the individual is tired, disinterested or quite content with situations as they are. Skin conductance and the galvanic skin response are the indices generally used to measure levels of arousal. Conductance gives an indication of an individual's normal level of activation. The galvanic skin response on the other hand gives an indication of an individual's temporary reaction in terms of activation when confronted with an actual specific stressful situation.

Individuals vary in their perceptions of stressful situations but in a sports context some examples might be: taking penalties in football, the time immediately before an athletics contest and set and match points in racquet games. Research indicates that arousal levels are related to differences in personality. Extraverts generally have lower levels of arousal than introverts (Claridge and Herrington, 1960) and neurotic people are more readily aroused when put under stress (Davies *et al*, 1963). The position is complicated to some extent by the fact that arousal levels also vary even for the same individual according to the time of day (Blake, 1967). Colquhoun and Corcoran (1964), for example, found that introverts perform better in the morning and extroverts better in the evening.

The relationship between arousal level and the performance of complex tasks such as sports skills is curvilinear (Figure 3). As arousal level rises so does performance up to an optimum beyond which performance begins to decline (Duffy, 1957; Stennett, 1957).

Figure 3: Arousal levels and performance

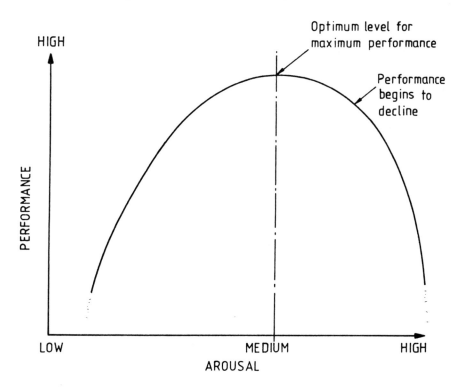

However, the relationship between arousal and performance as it is depicted in Figure 3 is generally not so clear cut. Mediating factors, such as ability, past experience of similar situations and the need for achievement, among other factors generally serve to make the relationship more complex.

Mild stress is generally associated with an improvement in performance as the individual becomes more alert and he therefore begins to respond more quickly and accurately to situations. However, on the other hand, severe stress frequently results in a deterioration in performance because at high levels of activation the player is too keen, agitated and excited.

Welford (1968) suggests that the intensity of motivation would appear to be an essential feature of the feedback mechanism which underlies skilled performance. In other words, the individual receives effective visual knowledge of the results of his actions. In optimal conditions of stress such knowledge not only enables a person to adjust his behaviour and to correct errors but it also has an activating and incentive effect. However, departure from the optimum propels an individual to action. As this departure from the optimum increases so do the efforts of the individual increase in intensity. On the other hand as departure from the optimum decreases the individual begins to relax his/her efforts.

An obvious example to illustrate this theory concerns the swimmer who suddenly finds him/herself to be too far out at sea. He/she decides to swim back and his/her actions will become increasingly vigorous should he/she find him/herself being carried still further out. On the other hand, if thankfully he/she begins to approach the shore his/her actions diminish in intensity as he/she reaches shallow water.

It is possible to elaborate from this simple feedback model to account for a number of situations in sport in which behaviour becomes more or less intense.

Competitions which involve 'racing against the clock' provide graphic examples of this feedback mechanism occurring in a sports context such as are seen in some show jumping competitions. Thus as the time remaining decreases relative to the tasks still to be completed actions are speeded up until with only a few minutes remaining the contestants can become engaged in a frenzy of activity virtually amounting to panic with a breakdown in skilled performance. One-day cricket matches in which the number of overs is limited frequently provide examples of this behaviour when the run-rate in the early stages of an innings is so low as to leave the later batsmen with an increasingly difficult target. In this situation there can be a lowering of attention reactions as a consequence are slow and skilled performance begins to break down.

Tennis matches seem to constantly provide examples of this

feedback mechanism in a sports context. Players who are in a losing position may sometimes intensify their efforts in order to remedy the situation. In cases where players are functioning below the optimum level of activation for successful performance this may serve to help a player begin to overhaul his opponent. However, where a player is already functioning at his optimum level of activation or above, any increase in this level is likely to result in a deterioration in performance. As players see the possibility of defeat looming even larger then this in some cases is accompanied by even greater intensity of effort. The intensity of effort in this situation is perhaps illustrated by the employment of rash strokes, by strokes born of desperation such as fast second serves. Sometimes players adopt quite inappropriate tactics such as 'net rushing' on a very 'slow' court. Thus there is a loss of concentration and therefore of control. Judgment is impaired and there is a deterioration in functioning intelligence. Put bluntly it is said that as emotional arousal goes up functioning intelligence comes down. This is sometimes reflected even at the very top of the game in tennis by court strategies which are naïve beyond belief. The situation is well illustrated from the comments of a world class Davis Cup player following his defeat in that competition in 1984:

> It was my fragile mentality again.
>
> For some reason, I don't know why I had no feel for the ball or confidence out there. I was constantly coming in behind some of the worst shots and also hitting some of the worst volleys.
>
> I knew I was doing it all wrong but I was so uptight that I couldn't do anything about it. I thought if I tried to play him from the back of the court I would 'choke'.[1]

For a player in a winning position the tendency will be to become less activated. In this case there is a real danger of a player, with a commanding lead, becoming underaroused resulting in a loss of concentration and the employment of casual, carefree strokes. This is not an uncommon feature among juniors or inexperienced players. The more experienced player, on the other hand, has learned to remind himself never to 'relax his grip' until the final point has been won.

Implicit in this theory is the need for achievement, and whilst the swimmer in the example related earlier never ceases in his efforts until exhausted, the losing tennis player may sometimes relax his/her effort because the need for achievement is not so great, or by appearing to be disinterested he may in this way attempt to account for his/her failure.

Competitive sport in this country is often riddled with exhortations from managers, coaches and trainers for sportsmen and women to try harder. 'Pep talks' for example have become a feature of most football matches before the game and again at the half-time interval. There is, however, no evidence to suggest that 'pep talks' have any value. Indeed, exhorting highly aroused players to show still further effort is counterproductive resulting in poor concentration and slow reactions. In this way footballers, for example, can become too agitated before the game even starts. Thus highly excited forwards often seem to be 'All arms and legs' exhibiting poor control and lack of quick anticipation which is quite uncharacteristic of their performance in practice matches.

'Pep talks' are in marked contrast to Galwey's theory of the 'inner game', which is concerned with maximizing performance in sport. Galwey (1974) argues convincingly that the secret of winning lies in not trying too hard and emphasizes the importance of having a 'calm mind' which he says results in spontaneous performance. Verbal instructions, Galwey considers, are likely to mean that a person will be over-trying which will serve to inhibit his/her performance.

Since activation or arousal levels have been seen to be directly related to performance the implications for the coach are clear. Somehow he/she has to arrange conditions which will produce a more or less optimum level of arousal in the players if they are to perform at their best. It is a difficult task, for players differ both behaviourally and physiologically in their reaction to competitive situations and the way in which stress is perceived. Thus some individuals are generally tense, others in only certain muscle groups. Heart rates also vary between athletes as does palm sweating. The position is exacerbated by the fact that a highly stressful situation for one player is not necessarily so for another.

It follows, therefore, that if a coach is to help his players in any way he/she must have studied their reactions over a period and in a variety of situations in the sports context. In tennis, for example, a player should be observed during practice sessions, in competitive singles and in competitive doubles. His/her play should be observed both on slow hard courts and on faster playing surfaces. He/she should be watched in play against relatively strong players and against relatively weak players. A check list of points agreed between a group of coaches will help to improve the objectivity of the exercise as will the opinions of others who have been in regular contact with the player. The check list would include items concerning attitudes and emotional and behavioural reactions to stress in addition to such things as technical skill, court strategy and general tactics. It is this sort of wide-ranging, thorough appraisal of personality characteristics which is needed to build up a useful profile upon which to shape a player's future training programme and the psychological advice and support to be given in the pre-competition build-up. It should be emphasized that the short casual observation of a player's behaviour before and during competition is likely to have very little validity.

Before proceeding to ways in which a coach can advise and create situations to optimize activation levels it is important to refer to factors which are likely to influence the extent to which any advice is heeded. Where a coach is seen to be committed and to have recognized professional technical skill and knowledge it is likely that not only will his advice be accepted by players but probably welcomed (Davies, 1980). The empathy of the coach is also an important factor for coaches who can convince players that they know what it feels like to be in particular competitive situations are likely to have more influence than those who are naïve or insensitive to a player's feelings in these situations. As with teaching, good working relationships are important and the development of such relationships will be facilitated where the thinking and attitudes of coaches and players are largely in harmony. From the foregoing discussion it follows that the approach of the coach must be individually focused and, since the optimum level of activation falls as the difficulty of the task increases, he/she will need to take into account the perceived difficulty of the contest for each player.

Certainly with respect to junior tennis in this country some young players view competitive events out of all proportion to their actual importance and the behavioural indications support the view that they are overactivated to perform at all well. Here a coach can help by putting the event in its proper perspective which will serve to devalue its importance. Conversely with players who are under-activated the coach can stress the importance of having a positive approach to the match and the possibility that it may provide an opportunity to further develop a player's ability. Certainly the perceptive coach will warn a player beforehand of the danger inherent of being complacent. With a player who is not sufficiently activated mistakes will arise from poor concentration and in consequence poor anticipation. This genuine air of complacency which is sometimes displayed by superior players should not be confused with the air of unconcern which anxious players sometimes assume. The latter is likely to be only a superficial veneer which an individual may adopt to cope with a stressful situation. It is an attitude which serves in effect to help a player account for his failures and it can disappear if he starts to do well. The coach should be aware of this attitude which could belie a player's real motives towards the game.

The perceptive coach will also be alert to the effects of failure upon the young player. Regular failure to win can be quite demoralizing for a player fails to gain the reinforcement which comes with success. Some anxious players may worry that they are letting the coach down and become over-anxious and over-activated before and during competitive events. It is important always for the coach to give assurance and also in this situation somehow to imbue the young player with confidence concerning his/her future match programme where this is justified by the young player's ability. If necessary the tournament programme should be adjusted so that the player has a better chance of success. A pessimistic approach is only likely to exacerbate the condition and lead to further loss of morale and confidence. It is important also that the coach should be aware that there are personality differences in reaction to failure. Continuous failure is depressing for most but it seems that the occasional setback can act as a spur for those aggressive, temperamentally robust individuals who may react to this challenge with renewed enthusiasm and vigour. So here too tournament programmes might be adjusted to include more difficult matches in cases where a coach suspects that his pupil is becoming unjustifiably complacent.

Oxendine (1970) suggests that with the paucity of evidence available in the sports field it is only possible to be speculative about optimum levels of activation for particular sports activities. However, it is evident that the optimum level of arousal does vary according to the demands of a particular sports activity. Relatively high levels of arousal are likely to be optimal for activities in which the emphasis is on speed, strength and endurance. Examples of activities requiring *relatively* high levels of arousal for maximum performance include sprint races, weightlifting, the shot put, swimming races, wrestling and the long jump.

For complex activities which require fine muscle control, coordination and steadiness then relatively low levels of arousal, though above the normal, will be optimal. Examples of such activities in sport include putting in golf, snooker, rifle shooting, archery, bowling, figure skating and in tennis the drop shot and stop volley. For these activities excessive muscle tension arising from a high level of arousal is a distinct handicap. When putting in golf, the effects of high activation are likely to be devastating with the putts lacking accuracy and precision being generally either far too long or far too short. A further problem for the competitor is that excessively high levels of arousal result in a lowering of concentration. The problem here is that attention can shift away from the actual sports activity to task-irrelevant stimuli such as the presence of the coach, officials, friends and observers generally.

Away from the stress of competition optimizing activation levels in practice sessions is more straightforward. Here the intensity of motivation of the players will be strongly influenced by the goals or objectives which are established. These must be meaningful and it helps if players are allowed to cooperate in their planning. Activation is likely to be optimal when the objectives are just within reach of a player's ability and therefore present a stimulating challenge. On the other hand, with goals which are too easy, a player is likely to become bored and disinterested and with goals which are too difficult the tendency will be for people to become despondent and eventually to give up.

The foregoing discussion has centred upon factors likely to influence the activation levels of athletes. These include the perceived difficulty of the task, the type of activity, the personality of the athlete and the degree of incentive present. Additionally such factors as an athlete's physical and match condition and the differential effects of particular social contexts such as audience effects (Cox, 1966) further complicate the issue. The weight and the way in which these several factors interact seem likely to vary from contest to contest and it would require a major clinical study to assess their relationships to activation levels even for one event.

With present knowledge it is only possible to set out broad guidelines for coaches and to recognize that an awareness of the affective dimensions influencing performance in a competitive athletic context will enable coaches to have a greater understanding of the emotional needs of athletes. Even if he is unable to manipulate conditions so as approximately to optimize arousal levels the perceptive coach may at least be in a position to avoid the pitfalls which engender underactivation or overactivation in the athlete.

Competitive sport in this country is often riddled with exhortations from managers, trainers and coaches for athletes to try harder. With activation levels high above the optimum for fine muscle control it may be true to say that, in a very real sense, an athlete can in fact be trying too hard. This is in fact a feature of much of English League Football with the pace being too fast for the skill of the players. Half-time 'pep' talks serve to increase the tempo still further and, as a consequence, over-excited and agitated players make simple errors quite untypical of their performance in practice games.

Conclusion

The acquisition of skill in sport will frequently be facilitated when the aspiring champion performer is essentially intrinsically motivated. Intrinsic motivation is immensely satisfying because it gives the individual a sense of personal control over the sports situation in which he finds himself. Intrinsic motivation means that the young person will be seeking opportunities to train and to practise even in the absence of being directed to do so.

Competitive stress can serve to disrupt progress and lower motivation (Davies, 1981). However, in the case of the intrinsically motivated performer, social considerations assume only secondary importance and thus the attendant stresses are correspondingly reduced. This means that the intrinsically motivated performer is in a relatively good position to handle the pressures of competitive sport.

Powerful motives which prompt a young person to engage in a sport are those of affiliation and personal excellence. Affiliation is the need to be socially acceptable and worthwhile. Personal excellence is the desire to be able to do something really well, to become highly skilled at a sport. Many young people take a great pride in their performance and there is therefore a continual striving for improvement. Young people also engage in sport for other motives though these are less strong. Other motives include the need for interest and excitement and the need for prestige, status and independence.

From the arguments presented in this chapter, the implications for training, practice and coaching are clear. Situations have to be created which will enhance intrinsic motivation and provide opportunities for the pursuit of personal excellence in sport. It is the pursuit of personal excellence which should be the dominant concern of both the learner and the coach. The practical application of these theoretical considerations, central to achievement in sport, are explored in considerable detail in later chapters in this book.

Note

1   The term 'choke' presumably derives its origin from the fact that a person under extreme stress can literally start to 'choke' through a tightening of the muscles in the bronchial system.

Chapter 2

Practice

Introduction

Since there are a number of books which deal with the technical aspects of this topic we have confined ourselves largely to the psychological considerations of practice. These are in some cases illustrated and supported by statistics from our independent research. The principles of the transfer of training are outlined and the dangers inherent in the widely used practice of half-court singles are pointed out. Guidelines for making practices effective are advanced and the importance of taking due account of the differing individual needs of players is emphasized. Anticipation is discussed in relation to the need for practice to provide relevant experiences if the development of this phenomenon is to be facilitated. The nature and value of mental practice is discussed in relation to its value both as a complement and as a substitute for actual physical practice.

The chapter concludes with a discussion of the importance of 'feedback' or knowledge of results of performance for anyone wishing to become a better player. In the absence of knowledge of results little or no learning takes place. Indeed, it is evident that knowledge of results is a powerful factor controlling motivation, learning and performance.

The first part of the chapter is devoted to the results of my research involving British junior tennis competitors. The conclusions which are drawn have significance for a number of individual competitive ball games and for most sports to varying degrees.

The adage 'practice makes perfect' needs qualification. It would indeed be more correct to say that 'practice makes permanent' for it is practice which is of the right kind which leads to the highest levels of skilled performance or as near as it is possible to get to perfection. Practising the wrong things, the wrong techniques, the wrong court strategies is harmful and can in fact be harmful to the extent that a player who engages in such activities could be worse off when it comes to making genuine progress than somebody who has not played the game at all, is starting from scratch but under expert guidance. This is because incorrect techniques and strokes have to be unlearned and it is well known how difficult it is to break well established habits. To give an example from tennis, a young student at college served the ball using what is known as the 'frying pan' grip. Although with this grip some progress is made, this soon comes to a halt and it becomes quite impossible to develop a service having any power, the ball being merely placed into the service court. Although shown the correct grip the student found it difficult to make the change, and when he did so his service became even worse than it was with his well-established 'frying pan' grip. It is important, therefore, to see that practice is of the right kind, otherwise bad habits are acquired which are difficult to overcome. In acquiring new techniques the old techniques have to be unlearned and the likelihood is that a player's game will get worse before it begins to get better.

Practice has to be strictly relevant to the full game. Surprisingly this is not always the case. In tennis, for example, one training activity which is a common feature of junior training programmes is half-court singles practice as distinct from 'knocking up'. Half-court singles practice could well be a classic example of negative transfer of training with strokes and strategies acquired in this context transferring to the full court situation to the detriment of performance and progress. In other words, players when they return to playing on a full court may continue to play the strokes used in half-court singles simply by force of habit. Extensive half-court singles practice also means that players do not have the opportunity to develop and cultivate wide-angled shots nor indeed have the opportunity of learning how to receive them. There are therefore clear dangers inherent in half-court singles and it is an activity which is best avoided. If singles practice is required then far better to reduce the playing time available for each individual to permit the use of a full court. The game will then be practised in the total context of the learning situation. This is psychologically sound for practice sessions should be carried out in conditions which are as close as possible to the real game situation. The author's research also shows that it is an activity which is not favoured by the young players, as Table 1 shows.

TABLE 1: Preference for seven training activities

	Activity	First preference percentage	Second preference percentage
1	Competitive singles against adults using a full court	39.0	31.5
2	Assistance and advice concerning stroke production	25.0	11.5
3	Pressure training	20.0	11.5
4	Competitive singles against boys using a full court	13.5	27.0
5	Physical training exercises	2.1	7.0
6	Competitive singles against boys using a half court	0.7	3.6
7	Competitive singles against adults using a half court	–	5.0

My own research indicates that not only the extent but the quality of practice are important factors concerned with successful tournament performance at the junior level. The research supported a popularly held view that to improve in competitive sport it is advantageous to practise with players of a comparable or superior standard to one's own (Table 2).

Practice with players of county standard was found to be highly significant for achievement at ages 14, 15 and 16 (Table 2). Practice with club players, on the other hand, was not significantly related to success in tournament play. For 12-year-old boys it may be that their skill is insufficiently advanced for benefit to be derived from practice with county players rather than club players.

TABLE 2:
Correlation coefficients for achievement and practice with county and club players

Age	Practice with county players	Practice with club players
12	.01	.25
14	.53°	.11
15	.34*	.07
16	.46*	.11

*significant at 5 per cent level
° significant at 1 per cent level

For those readers unfamiliar with statistics the phrase significant at the 5 per cent level means that there is only a 5 per cent possibility that the relationship shown is due to chance. And similarly at the 1 per cent level there is only a 1 per cent possibility that the relationship is due to chance. The probable reasons for the importance of practising with superior people is that players have the opportunity to improve their anticipation and to imitate and to model their play on that of the better players. In fact imitating highly skilled players is one of the most rapid ways by which to improve. This point is elaborated upon in the following chapter.

My research, which incidentally provides the only objective evidence available, also showed that junior players, if they wish to improve, should be practising all the year round. The results of the research (Table 3) indicate that winter practice for 12, 14 and 15-year-olds and spring practice for 14 and 15-year-olds were significant factors in performance. Commitment at these times is clearly related to success later in the year during the tournament season.

TABLE 3:
Correlation coefficients for the amount of play/practice at four age levels and tournament performance

Age	Winter	Spring	Summer	Autumn
12	.38★	.21	.16	.20
14	.55°	.40★	.21	.21
15	.33★	.41★	.26	.08
16	.25	.09	.01	.21

★significant at 5 per cent level
° significant at 1 per cent level

The results indicate the probable importance of winter and spring practice for players up to and including the age of 15. They serve to underline the impression that young players who are denied the opportunity for regular, sustained practice throughout the year start playing again in May at a generally lower standard than they had reached the previous August. So a valuable opportunity has been lost for the young player, not only to refine but to consolidate his/her skill. This sort of situation must be discouraging and unhelpful for morale. Sixteen-year-olds, apparently, are less affected by this disruption to practice, which suggests that their skill has reached a more advanced stage and is therefore more resistant to forgetting.

The likely importance of winter and spring practice points to the need for a considerable expansion in indoor courts. The need is emphasized by the seasonal variations in the average number of hours spent in practice and play (Table 4).

TABLE 4:
Average number of hours spent in play/practice each week

	Winter	Spring	Summer	Autumn	Overall
London area	11.2	16.3	21.4	15.0	16.0
Provinces	7.9	11.6	18.0	11.0	12.1

Seventeen-year-olds were not included in the report because of insufficient data. There was a return, however, from one young man in this age group who had gone to study at an American University where he could combine academic study with tennis. He indicated that he had been practising twenty-five hours a week during the winter and spring as against a national average here of 7.9 hours and 11.2 hours (London area 11.2 hours and 16.3 hours). This practice was wholly with senior international players. If this is in any way typical of the practice opportunities available then there is probably no need to look further for an explanation of the dominance of the United States in the World Class game.

Although ideally a wide range of effective strokes is a very clear advantage, probably the quickest way to the top is to have really good control and therefore consistency in maybe just a few very powerful shots. This means that you are able to 'hit through' players who although 'match tight' simply don't have the power to 'hurt you'. Nearly all the Wimbledon players, for example, have very powerful services. Boris Becker, Ivan Lendl and John McEnroe are names which spring immediately to mind in this respect. Pancho Gonzales, who dominated the world game for some fifteen years, and twice Wimbledon Champion, Lew Hoad, are examples of players from previous decades.

Time spent, therefore, in cultivating a really powerful service will be time well spent. Furthermore, this is a stroke that a player can practise on his/her own. It is the development of power which counts rather than playing endless singles matches which after a short time fail to produce any further benefit. A lesson perhaps can be learned from Johnny Hancocks, the Wolverhampton right-winger of the early 1950s. Although of diminutive stature he had the most powerful kick in

English football in the early 1950s with the possible exception of Ronnie Rooke of Fulham and Arsenal. Johnny Hancocks had developed this power through years of practice of simply kicking the ball as hard and as fast as he could. In this respect he stood out in the English game at that time.

The emphasis on competition means that far too much importance is attached to the winning of tournaments and matches with the result that young players generally become over-concerned about winning at a particular age level and neglect to develop the power and sophistication of stroke to be able to compete successfully at international level. The policy produces large numbers of compact, efficient, 'match tight' players whose skill, however, falls distinctly below that of world class. The lessons can be learned from the aspiring concert pianist and the emerging world class snooker player to give but two examples outside tennis. They spend many hours each day in practising and developing their skills and not going all over the country to engage in competitions. They practise and practise to the extent that they become almost incapable of making a mistake. A further example can be taken from golf where six hours' practice is the 'norm for the aspiring championship player'.

So the message for any ambitious young player can be summed up in just one word 'PRACTICE'. Try not to be too concerned if you are not winning very much at junior level. Although rather poor results can be depressing the player must take the long-term view and continue to concentrate on developing some really powerful strokes. Once he has a control of these and confidence in these, progress is likely to be quite swift. The player may be disappointed at not attracting the attention of the selectors but remember that Britain has not produced a men's world class tennis champion, nor indeed anyone anywhere near this standard, in more than fifty years. Fred Perry was Wimbledon Champion in 1936. Since then, Britain has not been represented in the men's singles finals of any of the major World Championship tennis events.

In the following chapters I emphasize the importance of having a plan, a programme which incorporates a series of clearly defined, objective short-term goals for the achievement of high standards in competitive sport.

What to Practice and What not to Practice

In an article a few years ago in *Medisport, The Review of Sportsmedicine*, I wrote that one of the major disappointments of the British junior game is that so many young players of promise fail to fulfil that promise. Progress in many cases seems to reach a plateau around the age of 16 or so with players even appearing to get worse. I theorized that one of the reasons for this situation was that players were finding the stresses and pressures all too much for them and that the game had lost all its enjoyment. But another major reason for the failure of our 16, 17 and 18-year-olds to improve is that they do not become involved in effective skill developing practices to anything like a sufficient extent. At the beginning of this chapter the dubious value of half-court singles was discussed but even when a full court is available the practice routines do not seem appropriate for the improvement of skill levels. For example, it seems to be invariably the case that players spend far too long just 'knocking up'. For players who have well-developed, good sound strokes having balls constantly fed to them is needless repetition of strokes already mastered. If the point is that 'knocking up' serves to permit players to 'loosen up' then this is better done by some limbering up exercises particularly where court availability is scarce. Knocking up is for youngsters still learning their strokes. For more advanced players to spend more than a few minutes of practice time in knocking up is pointless. They already have the strokes but need to practise these in the conditions which operate in a match where balls simply are not fed to the player. On the basis of the coach's observation the player should have a record of his strengths and weaknesses and how these are to be respectively developed and eradicated. It may be, for example, that he is failing to return very wide-angled balls to the backhand. In this case the strategy would be to give the player plenty of balls to the backhand gradually increasing the width of the angle as the player becomes increasingly competent. It is the systematic attention to the specific parts of a player's game needing improvement which can be considered as effective practice.

All promising players at 16 years of age should be following individualized skill learning programmes designed to eliminate weaknesses and develop strengths. These programmes will be based on the coach's observations of the individual playing in a wide-ranging set of conditions and his resulting assessment of the player's needs in terms of skill development. The programme need not be supervised by the coach but should be under his direction. It will need to be monitored and adjusted periodically in the light of progress.

Practice and Competition

Part of the time spent in practice should be given over to simulating competitive conditions. The more experience a player has of gradually increasing degrees of competition the better he will be able to cope and to manage stress. Gradually increasing competitive stress creates resources in the player so that he learns to control and to regulate his emotions. Practice sessions then should not be carried out in some kind of vacuum but should operate as closely as possible to the actual game conditions. Practice is then seen to have purpose and meaning and it helps equip a player both technically and emotionally for tournament play.

Practice and Anticipation

Anticipation is a phenomenon which is learned. Learning takes place through continual exposure to playing experiences which are relevant. Where two people play against each other over and over again throughout the year, for example, their anticipation becomes extremely good against *each other*. This repeated experience means that they have been learning what to expect and therefore so much of the game eventually becomes predictable to the extent that the players rarely surprise one another. If they don't play against anybody else, however, then their good anticipation will be restricted to their private game and it will be less good against other players with whose games they are not so familiar.

Because anticipation is learned it is important that a substantial amount of the time spent in practice is with players of the same standard. If anticipation is to be improved it is essential also that some practice time is allocated for play against people of a rather better standard. Plenty of play against players of the same class will result in improved anticipation for play at that level and below. However, to anticipate the play of better players it is necessary to have experience of playing against them — and the more the better. Some years ago the author was watching Mike Sangster, the British number 1 playing a good county class player at the Cheltenham Tournament. The county class player began to miss a few volleys and started telling himself to 'watch the ball'. The missed volleys were not made against particularly difficult returns but in view of the lateness of the volleyer's preparation they were unexpected. This situation occurs frequently when a player meets somebody of a distinctly higher class. It is not an uncommon experience, for example, for a player to think he has hit a winner only to be surprised and beaten by the return. The player blames poor concentration. But poor concentration is almost inevitable in the case of inexperience. To be able to concentrate and therefore anticipate effectively against better class players he/she must have considerable experience of playing against them. He/she must play and practise with them over and over again to the point where he/she has learned to expect the unexpected. The whole of Chapter 5 is concerned with the psychology of anticipation.

Mental Practice

Once a player has become proficient with a particular stroke, say a service or forehand in tennis, he can then benefit from practising it in his mind. This is a technique known as mental practice or visual motor behaviour rehearsal. The idea is for a person to obtain a vivid mental image of him/herself actually playing the stroke. In this he/she is not watching him/herself actually play, but is actually playing the stroke in a mental sense. The evidence (Suinn, 1980) is that for the skilled performer mental practice can be just as effective as actual practice. It is a technique which is known to be used by world class athletes, skiers and golfers amongst others and can be employed as an alternative to actual physical practice when players do not have access to practice facilities. It can also be used to complement physical practice. This technique is discussed rather more fully in chapter 8.

Specific Guidelines for Effective Practice

Planning, organizing and controlling practice sessions occupies a major portion of coaching time, and there are several useful guidelines that can be provided for the coach in order to help sensible use of practice time:

(a) The practice session should be conducted under as near similar situations to the game as is possible in order to develop the level of skill of the player. Obviously learning skills in sport requires certain prerequisites. It is essential that there is an opportunity to practise these in a context which resembles the game. In this way transfer to the actual competitive situation is facilitated. This aspect of practice is particularly important for the development of psychological coping mechanisms, which may be necessary in the game itself.

(b)   Research has shown that distributed practice is usually more effective than mass practice. It appears that sportsmen learn skills better when the amount of time devoted to practice is spread over a period of days. For example, fifteen minutes of practice devoted to a particular skill on each one of six days is generally to be preferred in the case of young people in terms of progress to a single session of ninety minutes. Obviously the amount of time over which a practice should be staggered depends on the skill being taught and the ability of each individual. This can be partially linked to the concentration span of the player, but the very nature of sports skills makes this principle important for the coach.

The practice session must be long enough to improve a particular skill being developed. There is a wide range of opinion amongst coaches concerning the optimum length of practice sessions but one or two things are worth remembering. Firstly, sessions which are too long can have a considerable adverse effect upon motivation, and in time can serve to reduce performance. This is particularly important where the coach is working on a technical aspect of a particular game as opposed to some strategy which is probably better experienced over a longer period of time. Included in this period could be sessions using video analysis, discussion of tactics, strategies and different ways in which a possible opponent might be beaten. It is essential in the long run that each player is taught to think and analyse for himself. Secondly, the practice session should be compatible in length with the physical and mental maturity of the player. This is very much an individual matter. It is, of course, vital before a big tournament and following a hard 'run-up' in training that the quality and intensity of the practice sessions be steadily diminished and the emphasis switched from physical skill training to psychological training which might include relaxation and work on developing positive attitudes and constructive moods.

(c)   Practice drills should provide continuous participation at an active level for all members of the coaching group. It is likely that learning will occur when members of the group or squad are engaged in some way. Drills will obviously be necessary, but those drills which involve most players working most of the time can be particularly important in a motivational context. Those players who may not be involved directly in the practice drill, could be actively engaged in analyzing someone else's performance in terms of weaknesses, strengths, strategy, possible correction of techniques and so on. In this way an appreciation of the basics of the game can be developed. This will always add interest and incentive to the coaching and practice sessions and this development of competitive awareness is critical and is useful in the long-term playing future of the young sportsperson.

(d)   Players should be frequently stimulated to improve the whole range of their skills during a practice session. When players begin to show signs of not attempting to improve a particular skill drill in practice then the practice should be brought to a halt. To permit practice of careless habits can have a detrimental effect on performance. It is useful if the drill itself can stimulate the effort to improve, for example, if someone is practising a service against another player a record of the number of times in which a serve was impossible to return gives a standard against which a server can try to improve. This kind of feedback can motivate the player to concentrate on improvement and this principle should be applied to the various drills used in the game.

(e)   Diagnosis and correction of faults should always be used by the coach in the practice sessions. Noticing weaknesses and mistakes, and supplying the player with possible corrective measures is a major part of the teaching role of the coach. He/she can give attention to a whole range of problems from the smallest to the largest, attempting to improve efficiency, fluency and precision of movement, so that the overall effect on performance is one of steady development. It is quite possible for the coach to devise drills which will correct weaknesses and during the course of these drills, the player must not be allowed to commit any act which in a game situation would result in a foul or penalty. It is only in the practice sessions that the coach can directly influence the manner or style of play, and it is here that he/she would hope to moderate the behaviour of the temperamental and difficult player whose performances do not match up to his/her physical potential and technical potential shown in practice due to this lack of control.

(f)   It is helpful if the practice sessions themselves are satisfying to the players. Sessions can be hard and physically demanding but if they are also enjoyable it is likely that the young person will be motivated to continue. A sense of humour can help the coach here without the sessions becoming too riotous for the objectives to be achieved.

Knowledge of Results

This chapter concludes with a fairly serious section dealing with the importance of feedback or of knowledge results both for motivation and the development of ability. The term feedback refers to both knowledge of results (KR) and knowledge of performance (KP). The aspect of feedback which is the concern of this chapter is that of knowledge of results. Knowledge of performance is discussed in Chapter 3. This is an area in skill acquisition which has been extensively researched and the evidence is quite conclusive and its importance is perhaps best summed up by Sir Frederick Bartlett who said 'It is not practice which makes perfect but practice the results of *which are known* which makes perfect'.

Precise, objective information concerning results means that the learner is able to see for himself how his current performance differs from previous efforts. The important thing is that he is now able to monitor and assess his performance in the light of any variations in training, practice and technique. Furthermore, when progress is seen to being made then learning is continually being reinforced.

Knowledge of the results of performance or feedback is indeed basic to learning. Bilodeau and Bilodeau (1961) concluded that studies of feedback and knowledge of results show it to be 'the strongest, most important variable controlling performance and learning'.

Classical studies by Thorndike (1927) and by Trowbridge and Cason (1932) serve to underline the importance of knowledge of results in terms of its information value. In the course of acquiring skill it is important for the learner to realize the connection between what he did and what happened. As Knapp (1963) said

> Knowledge of results serves as a guide to the learner in his subsequent practices and functions as a basis of selection of what is good in that performance.

In coaching therefore the main aim should be to use this information to improve the next response. Successful responses are identified and repeated again and again in order that greater precision and more accurate timing characteristics are attained. Knowledge of results means also that attempts can be made to correct inadequate responses.

Research by Elwell and Grindley (1938) and by MacPherson *et al* (1948) stressed the motivational aspect of feedback which apart from providing information concerning performance, also serves as reward providing extremely strong incentive to continue a task since it relates to the distance between a present state and a goal. This aspect of feedback is emphasized by many behavioural theorists, notably Skinner (1953) who are concerned with the role of rewards and punishments within the learning situation.

Welford (1968) stressed the importance of the specificity of the information which the learner receives. Thus the use of precise aids such as graphs and tables provide the learner not only with knowledge but are also important motivational devices since the learner gets some idea of standards and is able to see with some clarity not only his own progress and attainment but the difference between his own and the skill levels of superior athletes.

Performers of closed skills in athletics frequently have very precise information concerning the results of their actions. Both the runner and the jumper know precisely how current performance differs from previous standards. They are able to monitor and assess their performance in the light of variations in training and technique and additionally their learning is continually being reinforced. Precise knowledge of results for the athlete therefore is a powerful motivating force in maintaining practice over long and arduous periods.

Artificial Knowledge of Results

In most games also external feedback is generally present and a player is able to see the result of his actions. However precise knowledge of results is generally confined to accuracy of performance; the tennis player can see for example whether the ball goes in or out of court and by how far. He can practise serving at targets in the service court and receive visual information concerning any improvement in control. There are risks to this routine, however, because an individual may play safe and slow down his/her stroke in order to become more accurate.

What is generally not available to the games player however is precise, objective information concerning the speed or power of his/her strokes. He/she must rely on subjective viewpoint which from personal experience both as player and teacher is quite inadequate in terms of information and also motivation. The learner may have some idea that he/she is hitting the ball faster than previously but he/she cannot be certain and he/she lacks accurate information concerning this. Lack of knowledge with respect to speed and power presents a problem for both coach and player for it is the greater controlled power of his/her game which is the distinguishing feature of the world class player. For the tennis player, in the absence of expensive timing equipment situations sometimes have to be contrived which will provide the performer with information concerning speed. This can certainly be done for the service and probably for other shots as well. Several years ago I was coaching the service to try to increase its speed. The player served at a wall the same distance away as the net would be. Two lines were marked on the wall — one at the height of the net and another some feet higher, above which it had been assessed that the service would be 'long'. Feedback came in the form of the distance of the rebound from the wall. In this way the player was provided with fairly precise objective information concerning the results of his actions. He was thus able to modify these actions if necessary in the light of this information. Additionally learning was continually being reinforced and motivation accordingly was high. The speed of the player's service rose above two or three learning plateaux and the player was able to experiment and to select for himself the most effective technique. An alternative way of providing specific information concerning service speed would be to have the server practise without a stop netting to the court and then merely measure the distance the ball travels.

Competing against oneself as in the example discussed above is a valuable incentive which avoids the friction and anxiety which can occur when people compete against each other. Moreover, it serves to emphasize the knowledge concerning progress. Providing the learner with precise, objective knowledge of results in this way means that he now knows for certain whether or not he is improving on his past level of performance. It is, of course, essential during the period when artificial knowledge of results is being supplied that the individual learns to appreciate what particular action is producing the best results. Otherwise, when knowledge of results is withdrawn the likelihood is that performance will decline to its previous level since learning will not have taken place.

Not surprisingly most people find competition of the intra-variety interesting and highly motivating. I had first-hand experience of this many years ago when monitoring the progress of a group of 12 year olds with learning difficulties. All were illiterate and had experienced some seven years of humiliating failure. Assigned to a small special class they were given counselling and individual tuition and began to make what was for them fairly rapid progress. The teacher gave them a standard word recognition test and let each child know his score. This was given on a strictly confidential basis. With growing interest and confidence, this meant that there were almost daily cries of 'Can I do the test? Can I do the test?' from these now highly motivated children. They had become mainly interested, obsessed even with improving their test scores and seemed to be almost unaware that at long last they were beginning to acquire reading skill. This development had not gone unnoticed by parents, however, worried about the possibility of mental deficiency in their children.

Almost without exception the performance of young British tennis players for example tends to 'plateau out' at around 16 years, or so. To maintain interest and therefore progress young players need to be made aware that as they become more skilled, as they approach the limits of their abilities there is inevitably a slowing down in the rate of their improvement with more and more of the time spent in practice being needed merely to maintain current levels of efficiency. Thus a major problem for many players can be one of poor motivation. The situation is confounded by the fact that for most players the winter months are a serious obstacle to progress. Coaching and supervised practice tends to be periodic and there are periods of a week, two weeks, three weeks or more when a young player is on his/her own and responsible for the conduct of his/her practice. If benefit is to be derived from coaching sessions then the player must be practising between these sessions both to consolidate and to develop his skill. Winter practice has been shown to be related to success in tournaments (Davies, 1980) and it is a time when a player should be aiming to increase both the power and the range of his stroke repertoire. However, opportunities for practice for many players can be limited during this period. There is often a shortage either of courts or of players of appropriate ability with whom to practise which could also be an important consideration (*ibid*).

It is, therefore, important that practice sessions should be made as meaningful and interesting as possible. To this end it is essential that the learner has as precise a knowledge of the results of his actions as it is possible to contrive. The quality of feedback is likely to be a crucial factor in maintaining interest and in the continuing development of skill at this time. The general lack of precise, objective information could well be one of the reasons why so many young players of promise fail ever to achieve their promise.

The coach has an important part to play in assisting a player to relate his actions to the results of these actions. A prerequisite for this is that the coach must have a thorough knowledge of the skill being learned. Given that is the case the expert coach can, for example, help a player to focus his efforts and attention selectively on those aspects of the task requiring further refinement and, also, by providing a player with feedback concerning incorrect actions, the task of finding effective responses is facilitated.

People concerned with the player's progress may often say that he is hitting harder in order to boost morale. Such remarks may be imprecise and will be of little help to the player who is in doubt concerning the accuracy of such comments. Thus the value of objective knowledge of progress for the games player cannot be overestimated. It seems likely, for example, that a player with confirmed knowledge of his developing power is likely to become more confident, and it is almost certain that he/she will perceive particular situations as being less stressful than formerly because of his/her greater ability.

Conclusion

Competitors sometimes complain about having no luck. And luck can be a factor in match situations. However, perhaps it is worth recalling the words of the former American and British Open golf champion, Arnold Palmer who was often accused of being lucky. 'Yes,' said Palmer on one occasion, 'and the funny thing is the more I practise the luckier I seem to get!'

Chapter 3

Teaching Sports Skills

Introduction

This chapter is principally concerned with the psychology of coaching and largely consists of an examination of the role of the coach as teacher and motivator. The coach is seen as being very much more than an instructor in technical skill. He/she is seen as having a central part to play in the long-term development of ability and in the generation of confidence for the competitive situation.

The personal qualities and strategies employed by successful coaches are reviewed. Ways in which a friendly, warm socially invigorating climate can be developed are outlined. Such a climate gives young players a sense of security, of belonging, of being valued which frees them to concentrate their energies on learning the game or sport.

The coach must be working to develop positive attitudes and enthusiasm among the players, the aim being that players will be deriving increasing satisfaction from the sport itself and will be wanting to take in the activity for its own sake and for the sheer enjoyment which this brings. Assessing individual needs, goal-setting and the planning of skill development programmes tailored to the needs of individual players are examined. The chapter concludes with an extensive review of the principles and practices of reinforcement a knowledge of which is vital if the acquisition of skill in any sport is to be facilitated and not inhibited.

The Function of the Coach

A coach is expected to mould the theoretical and practical understanding of games like tennis into a coherent pattern if the individual is to develop his/her potential to the full. Expert coaching is an essential requirement if a player is to make substantial progress in the game. Expert coaching means that the coach has extensive knowledge about techniques, practice drills and training methods. The coach is the translator of technical knowledge and research into the appropriate training units, each with its own goal, towards which he/she helps the player to strive. He/she must be an able and involved teacher of the game, knowledgeable about diets, health, equipment, rules, other players and their performance strengths or weaknesses . . . in short, the coach must be everything! Equally important, in top class sport, is the ability to develop players from different age ranges and stages of development, to handle players, parents, teachers and others close to the individual and possibly, even to deal with the press and administrators at various levels within the game. It is this wide ranging brief which makes coaching so fascinating for many of the game's thinkers. To some extent the qualities found in the top players are also evident, to some degree, in the top coaches. This is particularly true in terms of analytical ability and the motivation to succeed. Of the many roles the coach undertakes, the main one is that of the teacher, because above all else, the coach is attempting to teach players things they could not do before, as well as to improve the performance of each of those who comes into his care. This chapter seeks to develop an awareness of the role of the coach as well as to identify significant qualities each coach should possess.

The Coach as a Teacher

It is probably this aspect of the coaching process which bears the hallmark of individual differences amongst coaches. Some coaches adopt an authoritarian or democratic style. Some are democratic generally whilst occasionally being authoritarian. Some have a high profile motivational approach whilst others are low key. Whichever stance the coach adopts as a teacher depends on the blend between the coach's personality, his/her background and beliefs. Generally, all that can be said is that successful coaches show a wide variety of techniques, mannerisms and personal attributes, but they all seem to have one thing in common, they have the capacity to teach, observe and organize players effectively so that an improvement in performance occurs. If a coach can be measured by anything, it must be that criterion above all else.

Educationally Sound Coaching

Apart from the development of a personal philosophy of sport each coach must follow several basic principles if coaching is to be effective. These include the following:

(i)   The background of the player must be determined. This consists of an analysis of basic ability and previous learning. In tennis it is most likely to be dependent upon previous playing experience and the mental and physical ability of the individual. Generally it can be ascertained through observation. Some formal tests of tennis have been devised, but it is generally better to observe the individual at practice sessions and in matches in order to analyze skills, knowledge and emotional patterns which each player demonstrates in the stress of competition. At the base level of coaching, the coach will probably be more concerned with teaching fundamental skills, providing drills, and developing new skills and eventually putting them into recognizable game situations. Skilful coaches are not only capable of assessing the current ability of a player, they can also envisage what the individual is potentially capable of doing in the future, providing, of course, that effective coaching is available. Some coaches of youngsters are particularly inclined to select players of too young an age, perhaps on the basis of physical maturity, or even on the basis of a regular opportunity to take part in a sport. This could be a mistake, and as yet there has been no scientific study to show any relationship between the performance of tennis players, for example, at a young age with ultimate achievement. It is quite conceivable that a number of potentially good players have been eliminated from the game by coaches who were unable to recognize the potentiality of the individual in their charge.

(ii)   The learning activity and skill drills must be appropriate for each individual. These skill drills must contribute to the eventual automatic performance of the skill in the game situation. Repetition is the essential requirement because it is only that which can cause skill to become automatic. A clear demonstration of how the skill is to be performed is necessary for the player to gain the knowledge of the required movement. It is essential therefore for coaches to understand this full range of factors which affect the acquisition of physical skills. This is dealt with elsewhere in the text. Not only must the learning activities be appropriate but, also, coaches must be aware of other influences on the player such as emotional learning, family ties and peer groups. Each of these can influence the extent to which any particular activity is effective. Coaches can often set by example the sort of attitudes and ideals which they would like to see in the long-term development of the player. Personal attitudes such as tolerance and punctuality are all examples of how a coach can influence the development of each player by setting their own standards.

(iii) Psychologically sound motivating techniques must be used in order to provide each person with the considerable motivation necessary not only to practise but also eventually to win. Stimulation may be necessary if players are to continue to improve their skills. Occasionally drills can become monotonous, and the best motivational techniques of all are those which create a feeling of need for what is to be learnt. The techniques have been illustrated elsewhere in this text.

(iv) Provision must be made for the individuality of each player, should a coach be fortunate to have a group of players in his charge. This awareness of individual differences has often been a key quality of the top class coach. The top class coach seems to understand how to handle different players, their temperament and personalities. Some players appear to need continual encouragement and praise, whilst others become much too self-satisfied with such treatment. Diverse attitudes can often be noted amongst training groups and different ways of changing attitudes and building better ones is frequently an area of attention for the insightful coach. The drills and practice sessions alone have to be planned to meet the varying individual motivational and emotional needs of the learners, if, once again, ultimate potential is to be reached.

(v) The ability to diagnose accurately faults distinguishes the outstanding coach from the average. The capability to analyze weaknesses or mistakes and supply corrective measures is a characteristic associated with successful coaching.

(vi) Learning and training must be coherent, recognizable and readily understood by each player if it is to provide any form of adequate motivation, which is the essential prerequisite to performance. Basic, or advanced skills only become valuable to the player when he or she understands how, when and where to use them in the game. It is vital, therefore, that the teaching of sports skills is done in conditions which are similar to the game situation.

This is not to say that isolated drills should never be used. They are often needed, for example, to develop basic technique and competency. However, unless drills are linked into the whole framework of the game they will merely become fragmentary and not be of maximum value. Perhaps the major characteristic associated with the coach for the development of these types of relevant drills is the use of a fertile imagination rather than the dependence upon well tried drills. Variety is the spice of life for both coach and player.

(vii)   The physical and social environment must be ideal if players are to learn from their experiences in practice sessions. It is of little use only being able to perform well on one particular pitch or court or in one situation. It is the capacity to adapt and to create in a constantly changing sports environment, for example, which characterizes top class players. Therefore the coach must not rely on too much habituation, if the environment is to be conducive to long-term learning. All good coaches seem to apply these basic principles with a flare that distinguishes them from the average coach.

Communication in Coaching

Individuals interact with each other through the communication process. In coaching, no single behaviour is more important than this process. Communication has much to do with the structure, the activity and effectiveness of organization, be it in coaching or any other aspect of human endeavour. There is considerable evidence to indicate that the communication breakdown between the coach and the player can result in a deterioration in the player's performance. Dealing with a communication breakdown is not a simple matter. Frequently it can be symptomatic of more basic difficulties within the structure of the training session or the group of players, or possibly among a group of coaching staff. The deficiency can only be overcome by improving the system. Sometimes communication breakdown can be directly attributable to a lack of skills such as listening or speaking. Most seem to occur because of the failure to understand people's behavioural patterns and the relationship between the source and the receiver, whether it be the talker and the listener, the writer and the reader or the performer and the audience, and possibly even the complex nature of the communication process itself. Since the communication process is frequently mentioned as one of the important aspects of coaching, some definition for the purpose of clarity and understanding is necessary.

Communication can be thought of as the imparting or interchange of information, thoughts or opinions using speech, writings, signs or other forms of language. By definition this conveyance must be between two or more people. The process aspect of communication is that it is a series of actions directed towards some end. These are usually continuous resulting in a steadily developing change or a dynamic interrelationship.

An analysis of communication reveals a range of types or kinds some or all of which may be as important to the coach and the player. This range includes interpersonal, intrapersonal, group, one-to-group, and non-verbal communication. In interpersonal communication, there must be a minimum of two parties involved and the exchange must be meaningful. The sender intends to affect the response of a particular person or group. The message may be received by the person to whom it is intended or by people for whom it is not intended or both. Depending on the communication situation, the message that is received may be distorted so that the sender's intention of effectual response does not materialize in the sender's expectation. For this reason it is essential that the coach in an interpersonal communication situation establishes that the message has been both received and understood and that a breakdown is not to occur between expectation and performance. Intrapersonal communication on the other hand is that communication which we have with ourselves in terms of listening to what we say, reading what we write, or considering what we think. In coaching, one is much less concerned with this aspect of communication than the interpersonal element. Group and one-to-group communication is actually a tool of interpersonal communication. In the group situation, it is important that the group is small enough for each individual to be able to communicate with all other members of the group face to face. These communication patterns within any typical coaching group will reveal that certain individuals talk with every other member/members, while other people avoid talking to each other. The coach's job is to establish communication patterns with each member of his squad so that ideas, philosophies and expectations can be effectively discussed to bring about the ultimate goal — the maximization of performance. The one-to-one or one-to-group is an important aspect of the coach's communication role. Occasionally he/she may be called upon to perform, or to speak in public; sometimes to instruct a group and sometimes to persuade, to inspire and to entertain. Yet the ingredients of the communication process are the same. Often when working with a squad, the coach will need to be able to switch from a one-to-one relationship to the group coaching relationship. This is a specific skill which needs to be mastered if the coach is able to operate effectively at all levels in the game.

Other aspects of communication which are seldom verbalized are expressions which might convey ideas, feelings or information or even attitudes to other people. Thus such things as smiling, frowning gestures, a pat on the back, a hand shake convey a non-verbal message. Research indicates that people are frequently unaware of the effect of these non-verbal messages and moreover are even unaware of the messages that they themselves transmit and receive. This lack of awareness can result in ineffective communication, yet interestingly enough, some recent research has indicated that some of the most meaningful expressions in the motivation of some players have been communicated at the non-verbal level.

A particularly interesting aspect of communication is the use of the voice. Research has indicated that each individual has virtually a unique speech pattern. This is a combination of two things — (i) para-language which deals with voice qualities such as tone, rhythm, resonance or tempo; and (ii) voice irregularities such as hmm! hey! err! These two combine with qualifiers of intensity — loud and soft, rate of speech — fast and slow, and pitch — high and low, to form the unique speech patterns of each coach. Most coaches who are experienced think very carefully about the way in which people hear their words and listen to the spoken message. For some it can be a natural gift; for others, many hours' practice in the coaching situation is necessary if they are to achieve this important aspect of communication. Effective communication just like effective coaching requires much more than merely knowing techniques or mastering skills.

The communication field is a broad and integrated one which becomes part of the daily life both personal and professional of each coach. Where group processes are involved, effective communication skills are particularly important in order to develop confidence respect, trust and cooperation amongst the people with whom the coach is working. There are obviously a range of techniques available to the coach in order to improve communication between him/herself and the player. These include:

(i) Make sure that everybody can hear what you are saying. This can pose particular difficulties on a windy day, and it is quite possible that the coach will have to move around the courts fairly quickly in order to make contact with all the players that he/she might be coaching.

(ii)   Talk slowly and clearly. Do not use jargon unless you are quite sure that everybody in the group knows exactly what is meant.

(iii)   Be concise. Think what you are going to say before you start talking. (In other words, make sure that the brain is engaged before putting the mouth in gear!)

(iv)   Do not feel that you have to be talking all the time. Research has shown that incessant talking is eventually 'tuned out', just like a transistor radio which is perpetually switched on for background music.

(v)   Avoid talking in a monotone. Modulate the voice to give emphasis, encouragement and praise.

(vi)   Teach positively. Do not just tell people what they are doing wrong with a particular action or in a game situation. Tell them what they have to do in order to correct the fault. This is a particularly vital aspect of the coach's communication role.

(vii)   Encourage people, but do not banter praise about indiscriminately when the performance of the player does not warrant it. Reduce praise to things which are meaningful to the player, thus when it is given its relevance is appreciated.

(viii)   It is particularly important to avoid destructive criticism and sarcasm. This can destroy a sensitive young player to such an extent that his interest in the game can be lost forever.

(ix)   A sense of humour frequently helps especially in a difficult session or one which is physically demanding, but the continual humourist can be extremely irritating, especially if the players are going through a hard training session.

It should always be remembered that the performer has to interpret the words into a physical action. Therefore you have to communicate in a way which is meaningful to the individual. It is here that the experienced teacher stands out. It is just not possible to explain how this is done in a few lines, but the following ideas may be specifically helpful to those coaches who want to improve their techniques of communication.

(i)   Adjust your vocabulary to suit the age group that you are attempting to coach.

(ii)   Find a simple repetitive description of what is required in order that you have a thorough understanding of a particular technique. Having done that, attempt to find different ways of expressing the same concept because something which is meaningful to one player is not necessarily meaningful to another.

(iii)   Many of the very effective coaching points are indirect. For example, a particular movement or action can often be achieved not by directing attention to that specific movement, but by possibly concentrating on the movement of another part of the body, perhaps immediately prior to the moment when the skill is to be performed.

(iv)   Make sure the person is quite clear in his own mind what he is trying to do. This should be established before the players get out on the pitches and courts to practise. Each training session must be preceded by discussion where the coach defines the objectives of the session, explains how these are to be achieved and then later follows this up with an evaluation.

(v)   Do not put too much material over in one coaching session. This can be especially important when coaching young players.

(vi)   Try to find words that convey what a movement feels like. Simple analogies from well known movers will help a novice player to develop. The more skilful player will have to use mental rehearsal and mental image to imagine what a movement feels like. Once the sequencing is established in his/her own mind, it is then possible for the coach to focus particular attention on that aspect of the sequence which is being performed incorrectly in order to try to modify the technique towards a perfect replication.

This discussion of communication and coaching techniques available to the coach, is merely a summary of a whole area of research, several aspects of which have been examined in other parts of the book.

Teaching Sports Skills

Basic principles

Most motor skills are learnt by trial and error and the extent to which the skill has been mastered depends largely upon practice. A simple skill like throwing, frequently repeated until we can throw accurately, is an example of this learning by trial and error. The problem with trial and error learning is that much effort is wasted in terms of time and energy whilst we are left appreciating the error of our movement pattern. Good coaching can reduce the period of time needed to acquire a whole range of skills in games and this is one of the basic purposes of coaching. So far as these basic principles are concerned, there are some which are of particular importance to the coach:

(i)   *Motivation*

It is well known that those players who are motivated will try harder to master a skill than those who are not. The soundest motivating technique is to create a feeling of a need for the skill. This can be done by showing how the skill is related to the competition, and by pointing out the successes of outstanding players who have used that particular skill. Motivation is such a complex area of the coaching dimension that the reader is directed to Chapter 1 for an extended review of the central issues of concern to the coach.

(ii)   *Early teaching*

It is frequently easier to teach and coach a skill if the games player has had no previous experience! Nowadays this is not so likely a situation as some children experience the game perhaps in the playground at school, in their own backyard or simply by watching television. The problem with these early learning attempts is that they may, or may not, have caused the child to learn correctly. The implication being, that it is quite possible for them to practise the incorrect movement until it becomes habitual. These habitual techniques, whilst incorrect, could have been learned and perfected to such an extent that they can bring the child some modest success. The net result of a change in this skill could mean a short-term reduction in overall performance in the game which, in itself, could lower motivation. This presents a problem for the coach who has to decide whether to break established habits and instil the correct techniques, or allow the player to continue to develop those habits which have already been established. Sensitivity and care must be exercised when making this decision because it may be possible that an innovation or development of the game such as the two-handed back hand in tennis could have been developed in this way. Experienced coaches often allow a style of performance so long as it is used with a high degree of success, providing it is not going to limit the ultimate development of the player.

Once again this relates to the coach's ability to analyze the best movements necessary to perform a skill, and to some extent this is related not only to technically correct movements, but also to an understanding of the individual player, for example, a knowledge of the fundamentals of biomechanics, physiology and psychology can help the coach develop his/her ability to analyze and make a decision concerning those movements which would be best fitted to each individual in his charge. That is not to say that there are no guidelines which could be given to a coach to help in this teaching situation. In fact these could probably be best summed up by the following three simple principles:

(i)   Each individual must be given a clear understanding of the inherent movement. This can be done by verbal explanation and guidance.

(ii)   The correct form must be demonstrated. It can be quite effective if the coach can demonstrate these movements, if not, better an experienced player or member of the group show correct form to the others. Excessive movements may look attractive, and be appealing to the player who is doing the demonstration. Generally, however, they will be counterproductive to those players who are trying to learn again. Video can also be used to give visual guidance.

(iii)   The early attempts must be very carefully observed and constructively criticized. The coach's role here is one of analyst and provider of feedback. He must observe the initial efforts of the performance and provide some guidelines for each individual as a way to modify his own attempts. Those who begin correctly can be praised, and suggestions can be offered to those who do not. If people are allowed to practise incorrectly, it will not be long before a complex habitual movement pattern has been formed that could take almost a lifetime of coaching to eradicate.

Preparation for Competition

There are some common elements in preparing sportspeople for competition and these include the following:

(i)   The player must be appropriately motivated for the contest. This is a complex area and is dealt with in some detail in Chapter 6. The major purpose of motivation is to stimulate individuals to perform at their best in a particular event. Therefore, the event must be seen in the context of the long-term development of the player and not necessarily as the ultimate test of a player's ability. A whole range of methods and techniques are available for this purpose and they are a part of the long-term psychological preparation outlined in Chapter 6. It is because of individual differences amongst sportsmen that the use of personal private comment to stimulate or relax can be, where appropriate, very important. This can only be achieved if the coach knows in detail how each player in his charge thinks and operates in a stress situation. Once again the best way for the coach to develop this kind of awareness of an individual difference or differences is for him to simulate those types of stresses in practice which are experienced in a match situation. Another alternative is to use a series of lower level competitions as part of the build-up to the big performance to develop the competitor's coping strategies.

(ii) The appropriate competitive attitude should be encouraged. Obviously the thought of the forthcoming competition affects each player differently. Some lack confidence, some are over-confident, some will need encouragement whilst others will need to be encouraged to be a little more realistic in terms of their own ability to beat the opposition. One particular way of usefully overcoming this problem is to stress the strengths of a particular opponent. Maybe even listing the number of times he has beaten your player beforehand. It can be pointed out to the over-confident player who is sure that he is going to win, that such an attitude can lead to a loss in concentration and thus poor anticipation.

(iii) It is essential that the player has a thorough understanding of the opposition. This preparation involves a knowledge of physical strengths and weaknesses, mental strengths and weaknesses and the emotional behaviour of that player in competition. The coach therefore, must do his homework, which is especially important prior to a big competition or tournament. Certain movements prior to a particular shot can be analyzed when the player has a habit of moving forward or backwards or prefers the ball to be hit hard at him in order to make an aggressive return. Full detailed match analysis is absolutely critical if the coach is to enable his own player to perform optimally in competition. After every match, the coach should evaluate not only how his own player performed but also how the opposition performed and the extent to which that matched up to his original evaluation. This searching of the self seems to be a particular feature amongst successful coaches.

Motivation and Coaching

It is the coach's own personality, convictions and motivational techniques which are of fundamental importance to the development of attitudes in the players which he/she coaches. It is quite possible for a coach who places a lot of emphasis on physical work to produce a player who is in excellent physical condition, and for a coach who believes in the importance of sound defensive play to produce a player with a predominantly defensive approach. Consequently, if a coach shows interest in one particular area, it may be that he/she could miss out on a total approach to motivation. In order to avoid this, the following guidelines are suggested:

(i) The coach needs to examine his/her own philosophy about what it is that he/she thinks is important.

(ii) He/she needs to examine his/her method of putting his/her philosophy into practice.

(iii) If it is not successful, he/she then must decide how to improve the situation.

(iv) He/she needs to be aware of how motivational techniques and strategies work at team, group or squad level and how this can affect the individual.

(v) He/she needs to attempt to determine whether he is unconsciously doing anything that might undermine his/her own, or the player's own motivational goals.

There are a whole range of variables open to the coach in a training situation which can help to develop the player's own levels of motivation. Whilst not all of these techniques may be of use to one individual, it is accepted according to Singer (1975), that the motivational properties of any activity and situation can be influenced through subtle or direct training techniques. This list drawn from Singer, whilst not exhaustive, may help clarify the training strategy which can be used to optimize motivation, and thus enhance performance:

(i) Help players set high but attainable goals. As has been demonstrated in the theoretical analysis of motivation, the level of aspiration is intimately related to performance. Some players establish realistically high performance goals for themselves which often reflect past successes and failures in similar situations. It is vital that the coach ensures that the player views his performances within a realistic framework according to development and potential as well as to the nature of each competition. As a result, in enabling the player to have a realistic interpretation of each performance, there is less chance of a player performing badly in a future situation due to a loss of motivation. Goals provide the player with something concrete towards which to direct his/her energies and, as they are specified, they can be evaluated. Additionally, specific analysis of performances are useful in that such information can be used to restructure the training pro-gramme should that prove necessary.

(ii)   The coach should supply appropriate feedback to the players about their performance. Information that could be useful in adjusting, controlling or regulating performances is of particular value. In many game situations, a sufficient amount of feedback can be present whilst the match is in play but sometimes it is the coach who will need to provide it at the end of a particular performance. Shaping desired behaviours towards a correct direction can be accomplished efficiently and effectively using reinforcment and feedback by the coach. This reinforcement can come in a variety of ways, although a typical example could be the coach's comment to the player maybe during or after a particular performance. It can be the coach's reaction to the player's performance, possibly demon-strating an interest and concern for the individual, or maybe using words of praise which can elevate motivational levels and provide the player with knowledge of the effectiveness of his own performance.

(iii)   Special strategies can be used in order to optimize motiva-tion. The intense and long period of time required in training in order to achieve top performance in sport, requires extremely high quality practice sessions over many, many years. It is essential that motivation is maintained during this period, and to some extent this can be achieved by providing variety in the training and coaching sessions. As far as pre-event motivation is concerned, the coach needs to analyze carefully the situational demands alongside each player's personality in order to determine the best course of action. The under-aroused competitor needs to be stimulated, and more commonly the over-aroused competitor has to learn how to relax and develop coping mechanisms just prior to and during a performance. These particular techniques are discussed in more detail in chapter 4.

(iv)   The practice sessions themselves should simulate the context situation. The arousal effects of competition are usually much greater than those of training sessions, but the good coach seeks to provide the competitor with considerable experience of stress in order that he can learn how to handle it. Not only should the sessions attempt to simulate actual event conditions, but also the coach should aim to allow each athlete to experience some contest competition prior to the major event, so that the competitor can build up a pattern of control and regulate his level of arousal to the optimum needed for peak performance.

(v)   The coach needs to be aware that each individual player is virtually unique. No application of induced motivational techniques can be intelligently applied without regard to individual differences. General principles about motivation can and should be applied. However, the need to be sensitive to the dissimilarity amongst players with respect to personality characteristics is essential if the coach is to get the best out of each one of his/her charges.

(vi)   Of particular importance is for the coach to foster a player's self-confidence and self-concept. The motivation for a player to persevere depends on the kinds of reinforcement he/she has had relative to previous experiences. A positive and realistic self-image is important. Positive reinforcement is a valuable tool in the development of a sportsperson's self-image, and a coach can control the situation in order that the probability of recognized achievement is present on particular occasions. Achievement does not always have to be evaluated in terms of victory, however, but it can be related to past performances and current standards in order to indicate relative levels of personal achievement.

(vii)   Training programmes should always be meaningful to the player. Those activities which enable progress towards the goal, constitute meaningful practice sessions. Activities which are interpreted by the individual to be relevant and related to goals are highly motivating and encourage an enthusiastic response. Frequently it helps if the coach explains to the athlete the underlying rationale behind the procedures, especially if it appears that some resistance might be exhibited on the part of the individual. Practice sessions are only meaningful when they are perceived as such by the learner.

(viii)   Intrinsic motivation is preferable to extrinsic motivation in the majority of sports situations. There are obviously many sources of extrinsic motivation in the modern game, available to both coach and player and many reward systems are in operation, the most usual of which in the professional game is monetary reward. However, the complexity of psychology appears to lead one to conclude that the development of intrinsic motivation will lead to more satisfying and long-lasting results. The feelings of fulfilment, expression and involvement will probably inspire the athlete to greater heights over a longer period of time than participation for materialistic gain. Extrinsic incentives in the form of various financial rewards, for example, can be employed to stimulate the young sportsperson but the effect of such an approach may well have only short-term effects. Ideally the major tactic of the coach should be to do whatever he/she can to enhance intrinsic motivation in which the individual is engaging in the activity for its own sake.

It can probably be effectively argued that in order to be successful, the coach must be present at virtually every practice session and that at each one of these high goals must be set for the player. It is the coach's job to build morale in the training sessions and a basic problem of any sport that involves repetition and periods of stress is to make the long-lasting practice situations both pleasant and enjoyable experiences. The highly motivating training programme often manifests itself by the manner in which the player approaches each individual training session. If a coach is concerned about motivational levels, he ought to study this aspect of the player's performance specifically in order to get feedback on the effectiveness of his training sessions. Depending on the type of person he is dealing with, for example, if all are intensely devoted, highly motivated people the coach can plan the programme without much regard for such psychological considerations as boredom. Conversely, if the players are not highly motivated then the coach's primary role must be to devise methods of motivating them. In the long term however, the player who, in a motivational sense is heavily dependent on the coach, will be unlikely to develop the competitive hardness required for success at the highest level in the game.

Research seems to indicate that motivation in achievement orientated activity is moderated by success, and thus the coach should set goals which are reasonably obtainable. More emphasis on self-improvement during training as opposed to direct competition with others may in the very long term be a more powerful motivating tool.

Coaches of top players have a special problem with many of the big competitions being spread out over a long season. In this situation it is difficult to peak players from one competition to the next. The coach must provide reassurance to prevent feelings of depression in the competitor in order to bring about the optimum motivational condition so vital to regular success.

Clearly, motivation is a complex phenomenon but there appear to be two components which operate significantly in competitive sport. Firstly, the desire to succeed has been recognized by most coaches as the essential ingredient for the player to continue with the training programme. Secondly, the fear of failure which has received less attention from the theorists, may also be an important component in preventing a player from dropping out of a programme at any stage. A third factor relating to levels of aspiration can also offer some clues to ways of motivating players in a game situation. Simply stated, the theory seems to indicate that individuals set specific goals for themselves and the success or failure to achieve these goals influences the selection of future goals such as more advanced competition, or the individual's evaluation of his own performance. Such simplistic treatment is inadequate and a much more detailed theoretical analysis is presented elsewhere in chapter 1.

The question still remains, however, concerning the practical ways in which the coach is to implement the theory in a training programme which will enhance the motivation of the individual members of his/her squad. Initially, it would seem that in order to motivate the young player to remain in the training squad, the coach should attempt to create in those who appear to be undermotivated, a desire to succeed. Level of aspiration theory may offer the key as far as motivating a less enthusiastic youngster by its emphasis on different levels of competition. Hopefully, the skilled coach who has borne in mind his educational responsibilities can, by setting suitable levels of attainment, motivate the less skilled and enthusiastic person to continue to strive for success, because sometimes, those who are beaten in the early stages of the game, may eventually have the physiological potential to become world class players.

Guidelines

1 Place in a very acceptable position, a bulletin board full of news, features and photographs of a game in order to maintain a general level of interest.

2   Try to establish communication links with parents through periodic letters or special parents' nights in order to watch an important game.

3   Produce a sports manual for each child which includes some statement of the coach's personal philosophy, some comments about regulations and standards in the modern sport or game and a brief theoretical analysis in order to try and promote the individual's interest in the game.

4   Have a series of individual awards. These are presented in a way which will give the participants a feeling of special achievement.

5   Organize all the practice sessions thoroughly, and explain why a certain point is being emphasized in terminology which each player can understand. Start all practices, matches and coaching sessions on time so that the players get used to a disciplined established routine. It is interesting to note here that as far as female players are concerned, some authorities seem to argue that the majority require the little extra extrinsic pressure from the parent or coach to add to the drive which is necessary for ultimate achievement of athletic goals. The view is sometimes held that as far as the female is concerned, gradual acclimatization, rather than immediate immersion, is the best way of introducing a heavy training practice programme. Probably another factor equally applicable to men or women who are involved in training for long-term events is the avoidance of boredom. Any kind of variation which can be brought into the training schedule such as different pacing intervals, variation in length of practice and environmental changes all contribute to raise levels of motivation. One of the most important outcomes women seem to seek in sport, it appears, is the opportunity for meeting people and forming a lasting friendship. This, it appears, is an important aspect which cannot be overlooked by the coach, and indeed, the coach should make an attempt to plan for specific informal social occasions. Another important aspect of female motivation is a self-image, and it is vital to maintain this if the girl is to become a long-term committed player.

In conclusion, the extreme complexity of motivating factors makes it impossible to make any definitive statements about which motivation techniques are best for people. The result of investigations seem to make it clear that there is a wide variability in the individual response to incentives. Individual differences need to be considered and the make-up of individual teams and squads themselves are often completely different. The successful coach must be aware of these factors as well as using his own successful motivating methods if he/she is to be a good motivator of sportspeople.

Reinforcement

Any behaviour or action which is followed by pleasing consequences tends to increase the probability of that behaviour action occurring again. Any behaviour or action culminating in unpleasant consequences tends to decrease the probability of that behaviour occurring again. Pleasing consequences which follow any action means that behaviour is being positively reinforced. Positive reinforcement can come in various forms. It can come in the form of self-knowledge or awareness in that the player is able to relate what he/she does to what actually happens. In tennis he/she may, for example, associate imparting spin on the ball with a particular wrist movement or a backhand cross-shot with stepping over further with his/her right foot. Positive reinforcement can also come in the form of the coach praising or acknowledging a good shot at the time it was made. Appreciation of a particular shot by other players can also be a strong positive reinforcer increasing the probability of the player being able to repeat this shot in the future.

In helping a young person to become a better player the principles of reinforcement need to be applied systematically if they are to be effective. The first step is to determine the factors which are important for maximizing skilled performance in sport. Goals or objectives need to be as specific as possible such as the cultivation of a 'kick service' a top-spin back-hand or a 'dink' return of service in tennis. In this way a player has something concrete or definite towards which to direct his/her energies. Additionally, where goals are specified, progress can be evaluated and the information can be used to restructure any skill development programme. Any advance which the player makes towards acquiring a new or improved stroke should be immediately reinforced and delivered emphatically to indicate its importance. The idea is to start with heavy almost constant reinforcement and then to reduce gradually so that reinforcement is only being given intermittently. In the later stages of learning reinforcement should be somewhat infrequent otherwise it will lose its value. Improving players are also being reinforced by internal reinforcers which emanate from increasing satisfaction and a pride in achievement.

The coach can reinforce a player's efforts in several ways. He/she can verbally praise performance by saying 'Good', 'Well done', 'That's much better'. Alternatively he/she might 'nod' or 'clap', raise his/her arms, a thumbs-up sign or whatever. The coach can also provide reinforcement by setting up targets or by measuring the speed of certain strokes, such as the service in tennis.

Organization

Organizational capacity is possibly one of the most important qualities of a successful coach. It would seem that there are four elements which must be the subject of exhaustive preparation on the part of every coach. These are organization of coaching material, organization of time, organization of facilities and equipment and organization of the players themselves.

(i) *Coaching material*

The material selected by the coach for each session includes all the necessary theoretical detail in order to coach effectively. An understanding of the physiological, psychological, technical and tactical components of a particular sport is of fundamental importance in the preparation of successful programmes. Well organized coaches know their players' needs in relation to the demands of the situation, and they can therefore establish priorities in training appropriate to these needs. It can be particularly helpful to the inexperienced coach to make a basic list of the essential technical, tactical, physiological and psychological elements involved in a game and to order these in a hierarchy for the purposes of analysis. This will be used not only to help the players, but also to develop an effective long-term training programme.

(ii) *Organization of time*

Any coach should be aware of long, middle and short-term goals in relation to time allocation. Long term planning may be over a four or eight-year period, or possibly over a year or a season depending on the particular level of competition with which the player is involved. The coach should consider the capabilities of his players relative to the priorities of his own situation, and plan his time and goals accordingly. The long-term goals may include an objective standard of performance, for example, the selection for a county team, or it may be a target in terms of a number of points against a particular player, or a more permanent objective related to identifiable improvement in techniques or of fitness level or possibly in a doubles situation. This principle applies to middle and short-term allocation of time as well. Middle ranges may include projective goals or peaking on a monthly or bi-monthly basis, but both should have a significant impact upon the utilization of the coach's time with his/her players. Short-term allocation of time on a weekly and a daily basis needs to be related to the short-term goals. To make the most effective use of the time available goals must be established in a hierarchical order. It is particularly important with a young player who might be involved in study which can affect his/her future career, that time allocation is sensible because it must be remembered that not all aspiring players will be able to earn their living from the game! What is vitally important is that the goals must be measurable by means other than a simple win or lose criterion. It is the opinion of some researchers that improvement in the physiological, tactical or technical component of the game will probably result in the improved psychological functioning of the player reflected, for example, in superior concentration.

(iii) *Organization, facilities and equipment*

The efficient utilization of facilities is crucial not only for the smooth running of a training session, but also for the general credibility of the coaching programme in operation.

To achieve this end, training or coaching sessions must be realistic in terms of their relevance for the development of ability in a particular sport. The competitive performance of the person is directly related to the training which the player undertakes. There is no denying the impact of the weight training machine, isokinetic trainer and the vast array of machinery now available, but in using such equipment it is essential that the coach keeps the realities of the game as the focal point of usage.

(iv) *The performers*

The final element of organization is the performer him/herself. Two main problems need to be considered, firstly, the organization must be such that the performer feels that he/she belongs to something which has a purpose and, secondly, is the importance of reality. Competitive sport can take many forms and it is vital that the coach identifies the essential elements of the competitive situation and incorporates these as frequently as is possible in the training environment. If a practice lacks reality it lacks credibility, particularly for the thinking analytical player.

Thus, these four elements can be planned before contact with the players is made. An important policy for the coach is to plan for everything which can be planned. Each element in itself is of critical importance in creating a coaching atmosphere which is conducive to hard work and ultimate success; combined together they create the framework in which effective coaching can take place.

Observation and Analysis

Probably the most difficult task facing the coach, especially at the beginning of his/her career when experience is limited, is that of observation and analysis. Clinical observation of rapid performance errors is not easy even for the experienced coach let alone the supplying of appropriate corrective procedures. Once strategic errors become the focus of attention rather than individual technical faults then the analytic task becomes even more complex. This is one of the prime reasons why the coach needs to have the sessions organized efficiently in order to enable him to stand back from the player(s) and begin his observational tasks without organizational trivia causing undue concern. Also, carefully planned practice sessions enable particular observational or analytic stances to be employed by the coach thus making it easier for him to fulfil this demanding and difficult role.

Successful observation and analysis depend upon a number of factors amongst the most important of which is the need for the coach to be constantly assessing the performer from a variety of perspectives. The position of the coach influences what he/she sees and a common error is to follow the ball without paying enough attention to the movements of the players. This skill can develop through experience but a self-critical thinking approach by the coach can speed up the process considerably, rather than merely relying on past experience and assumptions. The coach who evaluates him/herself as well as the player is much more likely to develop into an effective analyst of the game.

A useful general guideline is deliberately to move away from the detailed technical analysis into a more strategic position in order to consider fully the nature of the play. Patience and a willingness to let the play continue in order to appreciate whether errors are forced or unforced, habituated or random seems to be one of the characteristics associated with the best coaches in the game. Once weaknesses have been correctly identified then the coach can set about corrective measures drawing on the use of a wide variety of practice drills. Then, in order to evaluate the effectiveness of both the original decision and the practice the skill must be placed back in the full game context to see if it re-occurs. This type of analysis — isolation — practice — repeat game approach is very helpful for the coach waiting to develop his observational skills.

For those who are beginning their coaching careers there are a few general principles which should help in the development of the important analytic role of the coach. These are:

(i)   Watch the whole action to determine the major errors. Following the analysis of the action the related body action should be watched to determine the possible causes of any identified errors.

(ii)   Beginners will display random error so it is probably better to tell them what to do rather than what not to do.

(iii)   Once a fault has been spotted make sure the lead up movement is correct.

(iv)   Make sure beginners use appropriate equipment otherwise errors in technique may result.

(v)   Endeavour to instil a sense of coordination and timing in the early stages of learning the skill in order to develop the correct feel for the action.

(vi)   When coaching a group only speak to the person who is exhibiting the error and explain cause and correction clearly. Demonstrate correct technique rather than the error.

(vii)   Do not deal with more than one fault at a time — particularly with an inexperienced player. Ask him to concentrate on one major feature of technique.

(viii)   Short frequent technical sessions are better than long infrequent sessions, particularly if placed in the context of the game where the error is occurring regularly.

(ix)   As technique improves so can the pressure under which it is placed be increased. Too much early pressure, however, especially for the younger player, may require further analysis and correction of additional errors.

What is important therefore is for the coach to organize in order to observe and to acquire an experimental thinking approach to this particular aspect of his role. Coaching consists of the interplay between the elements of teacher, observer, communicator and motivator along with the important dash of individuality and flair. How the mixture develops depends on the critical stances adopted by the coach. This chapter hopefully has contributed to those in coaching who might not have considered their role in this particular way. The insights gained together with some of the guidelines provided should at least be food for thought for any coach in games at any level!!

Helping the Failing Player: Re-establishing Self-Esteem

An all too familiar situation in competitive sport is of the highly talented young sportsperson, full of promise who becomes disheartened through lack of progress and frustrated by temporary set-backs. In some cases, he/she considers abandoning the game or activity altogether. Such a situation presents a serious challenge for the coach.

Regular failure to win can be quite demoralizing, for players fail to gain the reinforcement which comes with success. Some anxious young people may worry that they are letting parents or the coach down and become over-anxious and over-activated before and during competitive events. Failure over the space of a number of tournaments and tournaments often leads to a serious loss of confidence. Adverse criticism in this instance is likely further to discourage a player who is already doing badly. The failing player expects criticism and hence this merely serves to confirm his beliefs. Pessimistic attitudes must be avoided for a player's self-concept, that is the expectations he has of him/herself will not only be influenced by his/her performance in tournaments but also by the expectations of coaches and parents and by the way they behave towards him/her. Where a player values the opinions of a coach he/she will tend to internalize what the coach thinks about him/her and he/she will in time begin to play to confirm those expectations. For example, if he/she gains the impression that the people responsible for his/her training do not consider him/her to be a 'match player' there will be a strong tendency to fulfil this prophecy with a player coming to believe that he/she has, in fact, a poor match temperament.

Players who experience a great deal of failure will tend to form negative concepts. They will feel that they are of low calibre and are likely to become apprehensive and uncertain concerning their ability. It is at this stage that they may decide to opt out of the sport entirely. Alternatively they may remain in the game but become mainly orientated towards avoiding stressful situations. Matches where there is a 50/50 chance of winning will tend to be avoided and tournaments will be selected where the chance of winning is either very high or very low. In both cases there is likely to be little stress for the player. He/she sees the tournaments as being either very easy or so difficult that he/she retains his/her prestige by avoiding blame.

In this situation the coach, whose knowledge and experience of the game is valued, has an important supportive role to play. Somehow the coach has to change a player's perception of him/herself — from someone failing to someone who can succeed where this is realistic. The coach should be seeking continually to enhance feelings of personal accomplishment and thereby to encourage intrinsic motivation. Successful attempts need to be emphasized and failing efforts de-emphasized. Success needs to be achieved in some area, in some event which demonstrates to the player that he/she can be effective. If necessary the tournament programme should be adjusted so that the player has a better chance of success. Most certainly the constructive advice, the empathy of the coach is likely to be of far greater help than the sympathy of relatives and friends which can be irritating quite apart from being unproductive. It is important to add, however, that the coach should be aware that there are personality differences in reaction to failure. Continuous failure is depressing for most but it seems that the occasional setback can act as a spur for those aggressive, temperamentally robust individuals who may react to this challenge with renewed enthusiasm and vigour.

The Qualities of the Successful Coach

As with the successful teacher, the successful coach likes people. He/she is interested in them. He/she closely follows the progress of his/her proteges as they continue to develop their abilities. Good coaches really enjoy social relationships and are generous in their appraisal and motives of others. They communicate a genuine, sincere interest and possess not only the ability but have a real desire to help. They follow the tournament progress of the players, not only in the newspapers but by their actual presence at a number of selected events in the season. They have the interest, the commitment, the desire to develop stimulating, warm, secure interpersonal relationships which are of crucial importance for the motivation and skill development of the players. They go out of their way to be pleasant and to help.

The successful coach is enthusiastic, concerned and creative in designing training schedules to meet the needs of individual players. He is well-organized and conscientious. He is genuinely interested in coaching and has a personal regard for the players. He creates a stable, relaxed environment to which young players feel they can belong. This is very important for the need for affiliation to a group or squad is very strong in most young players.

The style of leadership adopted by the coach is a potent factor, not only for the development of ability but for the general morale of the squad. An over-critical pessimistic approach with the emphasis being on fault-finding has a depressive effect. If this is coupled with boring, pointless, seemingly meaningless, practice routines and drills it can quickly lead to players coming to dislike the game. First impressions often have a lasting effect and if youngsters find little enjoyment in their first experiences of any sport they can be 'put off' the activity for life. Excessive competition and rivalry, for example, can quickly cause people to have an aversion for the activity or the game, particularly if they are continually placed in situations where they feel threatened and their prestige is at stake.

The overriding aim must be to create a happy, secure, emotional climate through interesting and exciting training activities and through satisfying, consistent, harmonious, personal relationships to the extent that young players will simply want to play games more and more.

To this end, therefore, it is important for the coach to create successful situations and to organize skill activities which are seen to be directly related to goals. Young people want to improve their game, they want to improve their technique and skill but are often not sure even at the age of 16 or so, how this is to be done. If the emphasis is on results, rather than the analysis of strengths and weaknesses, then playing endless singles against the same people is not the answer. Successful efforts by players need to be emphasized and failing efforts de-emphasized. The coach should be continually endeavouring to enhance feelings of personal accomplishments and to encourage intrinsic motivation. In tennis at doubles practices, for example, the importance of a player's contribution should be emphasized at all times. The role of the non-receiver in helping to break service should be stressed particularly with respect to exploiting any service return made by his/her partner.

Additionally the coach needs to be a confident, stable person who can generate an air of optimism and feelings of self-confidence among his/her players. He/she must be committed and, moreover, must be seen to be committed by his/her young clients. He/she must be able to diagnose or assess a player's needs both in terms of his/her technical skill and psychological, mental and emotional states. A good coach will really get to know a player as a person for only by doing this can he/she really expect to be of very much help.

A knowledge of the player is important from the motivational point of view, for what motivates one player doesn't necessarily motivate another. With some knowledge of a player as a person the coach will have a better idea of how to handle a player and this knowledge will also be important when it comes to setting up an individualized skill development programme. To come to know a player as a person means that the player's behaviour must be closely watched over a period of time.

The good coach then will be observing the player in a variety of situations. It is, of course, essential that he/she sees the player performing in various competitive situations and his/her reactions to these situations. Certainly it is not sufficient for the coach just to take coaching sessions and leave it at that. Such an attitude is frankly virtually immoral. For the coach to rely on the results of matches is simply not sufficient. Although winning matches at tournaments is the yardstick by which progress is measured it is far from being an accurate one. What matters most is *how* matches are won or lost. The safety first defensive player in tennis, for example, wins on slow hard courts largely because of his opponent's errors rather than his own winning shots. He wins with a game which may go as far as county level but will certainly fail to go beyond.

Unfortunately it is invariably the case that the junior player with ambitious, promising attacking strokes though not yet fully under control, who loses at the junior stage. But it is this kind of player who has the potential to succeed at higher levels and to make genuine progress.

Conclusion

In this chapter we have emphasized the crucial role which the coach can play in the development of the young sportsperson. Left to their own devices and unsupported, most youngsters will achieve very little. The traditional technical qualities of competent coaching, including instruction, guidance, organization and observation and analysis, have been examined and illustrated in detail. More recently it has been shown, however, that coaching effectiveness is very largely dependent on the ability of the coach to relate appropriately to the individual people in the group. We have given this concern considerable attention, not only in this chapter but in various sections throughout the text. The ability to relate appropriately to learners is a quality which is of crucial importance for enjoyment, for the enhancement of intrinsic motivation and thus ultimately for a high level of achievement in competitive sport.

Chapter 4

Anxiety, Stress and Performance

Introduction

This chapter looks at the relationship between anxiety, stress and performance. It looks at the various sources of stress and a detailed, comprehensive review is given of the techniques and strategies employed in the management of competitive stress. These can be used, where appropriate, in the instruction of individualized programmes designed to meet the needs of stress-prone competitors.

Trait and State Anxiety

Anxiety is viewed as an enduring personality factor or trait referred to as A — trait. This is the extent to which an individual is generally anxious in most situations. It is the latent disposition to behave in a more or less anxious way under stress. Anxiety is also viewed as a temporary state, A — state which is the anxiety evoked by particular situations. State anxiety refers to the subjective feelings of anxiety which an individual experiences in particular situations which are perceived as threatening, irrespective of the actual danger present. Interactions between the enduring personality factor A — trait and the temporary situational factor A — state occur and a high level of trait anxiety generally predisposes individuals to have elevated A — state anxiety levels in situations which are perceived as stressful and threatening to their prestige and self-esteem. Thus in competitive sports situations the high-trait anxiety person is frequently more likely to experience feelings of high-state anxiety than is likely in the low-trait anxiety person. Much depends, however, on how an individual actually interprets particular competitive situations. His interpretation will be influenced by a number of factors such as past experience, ability and training in the management of stress. These considerations, which are essential to performance in competitive sport, are examined both in this chapter, and also in later chapters, of this book.

Anxiety and Performance

Anxiety can be a major problem for many sportspersons, particularly for those engaged in individual sports and for those in 'exposed' or isolated positions in team sports such as goalkeepers in football and hockey for example. The relationship between anxiety and perform-ance has received extensive investigation over many years. The classical studies were carried out by the Americans Yerkes and Dodson in 1908 and their findings verified by numerous subsequent researches. These show that there is an optimum level of anxiety for maximum performance with both low and high levels of anxiety being associated with relatively poor standards of play. Performance improves up to an optimum beyond which there is a decline. The relationship, however, is generally not so simple. A player's level of anxiety is likely to vary according to how difficult and how important he/she considers a particular match to be. Thus, more able players are likely to be less adversely affected by the inhibiting effects of high anxiety than inferior players because they perceive matches as being relatively less difficult. It was Sigmund Freud who stressed the anticipatory nature of anxiety. We are anxious 'lest something occur'. Thus in sport competitors expect to succeed at some events and fail at others. Even before a game begins, therefore, they become more or less anxious according to whether they expect to succeed or fail.

In several respects a high level of anxiety is disadvantageous for optimum performance in competitive sport. Anxious people, for example, generally do less well in the important events than they do in the less important ones and in practice situations. It is also the case that anxious sportspeople are more adversely affected by failure than are people of a more stable disposition.

Anxious people generally ascribe failure to their lack of ability. They blame themselves for defeat. In contrast, people of a robust, stable disposition tend to believe that failure in their case can be put down to lack of effort. Thus, following failure, stable people respond in a positive way with greater effort and commitment, whereas anxious people tend to respond in a very negative way and to spend even more time worrying about their inadequacies.

Anxious individuals also do worse than stable people when the need to succeed has been over-emphasized. Novel situations such as a high wind, a different surface, an opponent with an unorthodox technique, create problems for the anxious competitor. He takes longer to adjust to become oriented to the demands of the situation. New situations give rise to uncertainty. There can be doubt about knowing what to do, about what is expected, about what is the correct course of action. Thus novelty for the anxious competitor frequently becomes equated with difficulty. The 'climate' of the particular competitive situation can also operate to depress the performance of the anxious individual. Officialdom in the presence of a referee, umpire, linesmen at tennis matches, for example, creates a 'strict' as distinct from a friendly, relaxed atmosphere and the greater such test-like characteristics, which serve to dramatize the importance of the occasion, the worse will anxious people perform.

Thus the anxious person is frequently handicapped in several ways in competitive sport situations. Although there are instances of people who have said that they felt nervous before an event and yet still went on later to give a good performance, Bell (1983) in his book *Championship Thinking in Sport* considers that such people perform well 'in spite of their anxiety'. It is in fact the case that a high level of pre-competition anxiety serves to depress performance (Hall and Purvis, 1978).

Anxiety, therefore, is a central factor in performance in competitive sport. It is a frustrating and depressing experience for the committed and talented youngster whose performance virtually disintegrates in competitive situations as a result of over-anxiety. There are almost daily instances of young competitors whose performance in match play fails to do justice to their ability, whose results are virtually incompatible with talent and promise.

Much anxiety is avoidable if competitors are sufficiently mature and prepared emotionally and if the emphasis is on learning and enjoyment. Regrettably this is frequently not the case. Writers in the field of sports psychology, Odom and Perrin (1985), refer to youngsters being emotionally 'burnt out' as the result of the psychological demands of competitive sport. Training policies, for example, which expose people to continual competitive play frequently generate a very high level of quite unnecessary stress which can eventually undermine the confidence of even the temperamentally robust.

This is particularly likely to be the case when undue importance is attached to the results of competitions. In this situation there is a real risk of young people losing all enjoyment for a game as many in fact do (Davies, 1981). It shouldn't really matter very much, for example, who is the under-12 tennis champion of Bognor Regis or anywhere else for that matter and yet everybody gets on tenterhooks and the court is surrounded by anxious parents and friends and with officials making snap judgments about a player's 'potential' on quite inadequate evidence.

Prevention is really preferable to cure. Particularly is this so with beginners when the negative effects of anxiety are most apparent (Martens, 1977). The problem is that young players can become *conditioned* to feeling anxious in competitive situations and performance obviously suffers. However, competitive anxiety can be treated. Effective measures exist for the management of stress and the reduction of anxiety. These measures are discussed fully towards the end of this chapter.

Causes of Anxiety

One of the most potent causes of anxiety is the fear of failure, which would be accompanied by loss of prestige and by feelings of humiliation. It is also the case that the more keen a player is to win the more anxious he/she will become. Tennis players, like everybody else, are anxious not to repeat humiliating situations. At junior level older players may become anxious about the possibility of losing to a much younger boy or girl or to somebody of inferior status. These are but two instances of situations in which young players may justifiably feel that they have nothing to gain but everything to lose in terms of status and prestige. This threat can become a very real one, even for the superior performer when he is faced, for example, with a relatively 'light-weight' but sound defensive opponent in a match played on a slow asphalt court. On such a surface the slow bounce of the ball means that positive attacking strokes are not only difficult to execute but their effects largely nullified. The margin of error is too small and a defensive, almost 'pat-ball' type of game tends to 'pay-off'. Such a surface favours the defensive, negative player and at the same time mitigates against the positive player. Almost inevitably there is frequently a regression in skilled performance. This situation is not uncommon in Britain since so much play does take place on asphalt courts. Promising stroke players understandably lose confidence in such conditions and their anxiety is often manifest.

Highly skilled seasoned campaigners are less likely to become anxious and their performance adversely affected by the fear of failure since they have learned how to cope with such situations and have become adjusted to dealing with them. But even they are not invulnerable to such pressures. There was, for example, the obvious alarm felt by the professionals at the first open tournament to be held in this country at Bournemouth in 1969. Pancho Gonzales lost to young Mark Cox fresh out of the University of Cambridge and the great Australian professional Fred Stolle in trouble in an early round match against an 'unknown' from the amateur ranks is reported as saying that during the match he kept on seeing the newspaper headlines from New York to Sydney announcing the news of his defeat.

For the anxious young player the position is likely to be made worse if parents or coaches are themselves over-anxious. Anxiety readily transmits from person to person and young people when parents or coaches are anxious will be fully aware of this. At tournaments anxious parents are readily identified by the obvious signs of agitation which they frequently display. Some parents are so apprehensive that they cannot bear to watch and hide away. One parent was notorious for doing this. He would usually secrete himself behind a wall or a tree or bush. But his son always knew that he was in hiding somewhere near the court. Such behaviour by parents inevitably increases anxiety in the young player since it conveys an impression not of confidence but one of doubt and apprehension.

Fathers and mothers can, of course, be far too ambitious for their children. Parents, by attaching too much importance to achievement in sport, clearly increase the stress and the anxiety for the young player. It is a similar situation to that faced by the children of over-anxious parents at the 11+ examination. The social pressures which are generated are sometimes so great that it is not unknown for young people to be physically sick before a tournament. Thus the anxiety and over-concern of parents is likely to heighten the anxiety of the young person probably to the detriment of tournament performance.

Perhaps unsuspectingly young people do worry about letting people down in competitive situations. Davies (1986) found, for example, that the two major sources of worry which students experienced during 'A' level examinations were 'letting people down' and 'past failures'. Nearly a fifth of the candidates reported that their concentration was adversely affected by these two particular worries.

A major cause of anxiety is uncertainty and doubts concerning progress and ability. With respect to tennis, young players can often be in doubt concerning whether they are continuing to improve. Athletes have the benefit of objective measures of progress which are not easily available to the tennis player. It would greatly assist morale, for example, if a young person had some evidence that he/she was currently serving or driving harder than formerly; as it is young tennis players can be 'in limbo' concerning their progress in the game. This uncertainty can lead to anxiety among those players whose tournament results are regarded as mediocre.

High levels of anxiety tend to be generally associated with feelings of insecurity, with over-caution and with indecision. Discomforting emotional feelings may also be accompanied by a variety of psycho-somatic symptoms. These can include sweating, headache, pallor, palpitations and nausea. Buster Mottram was actually physically sick at the back of the court at Wimbledon on one occasion.

Anxiety: Performance Characteristics

In competitive situations the anxious person tends to become over-aroused, too tense, too worried in fact to do well. There is almost inevitably a feeling of inadequacy and a loss of confidence. Thus in competitive tennis matches, for example, anxious players are likely to be rather hesitant and to have difficulty in adapting to new situations such as a different court surface or an opponent whose strokes, although unorthodox, are nonetheless effective. The game of the highly anxious player tends to be rigid, inflexible, stereotyped and is easily predictable. The highly anxious person is slower to react in the stressful competitive situation than he is in the relatively relaxed conditions of practice. At tense, crucial moments during a match the game of the over-anxious individual is characterized by indecision and, to use the language of the game, errors are made which are 'unforced'; a good example of this being the double-fault. Anxiety affects players in different ways. Some become tense and rigid, others become very active but in an ineffective way with players frequently becoming overcon-cerned with their own performance. Further, they tend to be easily distracted by stimuli which should be irrelevant such as the presence of spectators and hitherto unnoticed faults in their racquets or in the courts, for example. Concentration becomes sometimes so poor that players fail to perceive glaring weaknesses in the opponent's game. In tennis, there are even instances known to the author of young players failing to recognize that their opponents were left-handed! All this means that the over-anxious player, without psychological help, is likely to be seriously handicapped in the stressful conditions of competitive sport.

Stress

Introduction

Stress can be viewed as a way of testing a person to see just 'how much he can take' much in the same way as new machines are tested for power and endurance. In fact stress originally was essentially an engineering term but more recently it is increasingly referred to in the context of the physical and psychological demands which are made upon people. Stress, however, is difficult to define. This is because individuals vary markedly in their reactions to particular situations. Reactions vary because of differences in temperament, abilities, past experience of similar situations and motivation. The prospect of facing any one of the following situations would produce varying reactions among people causing, at the extreme, alarm to some whilst leaving others relatively unconcerned:

> Climbing a rock face;
> An audition;
> Making a public speech;
> Taking a driving test.

Thus it is more helpful to talk in terms of perceived stress. It is how a person interprets a particular situation which determines the degree of stress. It is quite possible for example that situations which pose a threat to a person's self-esteem, prestige, and status can evoke feelings of greater anxiety than situations which involve the risk of actual physical harm. It follows, therefore, that the more importance an individual attaches to an event, the more keen he/she is to succeed the greater is the stress for that person. Competitive situations, such as sporting events, are stressful when they are perceived as posing a threat to an individual's standing in the game or activity. The position is complicated by the fact that the perception of stress even for the same competitor can vary from one event to another and even over time for one and the same event.

Stress can be considered from two standpoints. It can be viewed from an individual's reaction to stress and it can also be viewed with respect to the source of stress. When the source of stress is referred to, the terms stressor or stress agent are generally used. Stressful agents in sport include spectators and incentives, such as rewards, which may come in the form of prizes and prestigious recognition at national, county and club level. Increasing the incentive, increasing the importance of the event for the individual increases the stress.

In the absence of appropriate preparation, stress reactions are likely to be experienced by individuals for any competition which is seen as challenging and which is clearly going to require much more than ordinary effort. The degree of stress will be closely related to the perceived demand of the match or event and the competitor's assessment of his/her own capabilities. For highly motivated competitors, as distinct from those resigned to the situation, the greater the gap between the perceived demands of the match or event and the competitor's assessment of his/her abilities, the greater will be the anxiety and pressure.

For coaches, trainers and competitors seeking to develop and to employ stress management strategies and techniques, it is helpful in the first instance to make a brief survey of the main physiological, emotional, behavioural and cognitive and attentional responses to stress.

Physiological Responses

Typical bodily responses to stress include an increase in muscular tension, nausea, headaches, stomach cramps, rapid heart rate, shortness of breath, sweating, trembling hands and shaking legs among others. These are indications that the body is preparing itself for action. Several of these responses can be measured. These include heart rate, blood pressure and sweating and can provide important objective information concerning a person's reaction to particular stressors. There are marked individual variations in bodily reactions to stress which underlines the need to have a battery of objective measures in addition to subjective reports in order to have a reasonably accurate indication of the degree to which an individual is affected. Heart rate for example may rise sharply in some people whilst for others there is only a slight increase. The extent to which people sweat also varies and although breathing is generally rapid and shallow even this response is not universal. However, the important point is that although people vary considerably in their bodily responses to stress the responses for one and the same person are closely consistent over time to the extent that it is quickly evident to others who know the person well that he/she is worried and apprehensive about the future outcome of the contest.

Discomforting bodily symptoms of stress are themselves a source of worry. Excessive muscular tension means that motor tasks are performed less well. People also tire more easily since more energy is dissipated. Physical discomfort is therefore likely to depress performance through a lowering of concentration and through fatigue.

Behavioural and Emotional Responses

An individual's perception of a stressful or threatening situation usually results in increased anxiety accompanied by an elevation in physiological indices of arousal. Emotional reactions to stress which exceed an individual's tolerance level are unpleasant. In a competitive sports context, an individual can be beset by a whole variety of discomforting feelings including guilt, remorse, uncertainty and self-doubt, helplessness, insecurity and inadequacy. Feelings of frustration can in turn lead to inward and outward expressions of anger — that is to say the individual becomes angry with himself and angry with other people. In this emotional state concentration inevitably deteriorates with the competing player being distracted from his task by his anger. Energy is dissipated needlessly in a situation in which all a player's efforts should be concentrated on the game in hand. In tennis tournaments, for example, the behaviour of some players is such that penalty points have now been introduced in an effort to control outbursts of temper which involve abusive conduct, towards both officials and equipment.

Typical behavioural reactions include restlessness, fidgeting, clenching of the jaw and a general tenseness. People can become agitated to the extent that at the extreme there are even feelings of panic.

Stress and Performance

Generally people perform best under intermediate conditions of stress. It is at the two extremes of high and low levels of stress that individuals do least well. This is because the introduction of stress to a learning situation in the form of a more difficult task or of various incentives involves action of the autonomic nervous system with an increase in the level of arousal. Arousal refers to the degree of intensity of effect or the intensity of emotion. As with anxiety, performance improves as arousal level increases up to an optimum, following which it begins to decline. Peformance improves as arousal level increases because the individual becomes more alert and can respond to events more quickly and more accurately. Thus mild stress leads to an improvement in performance. Severe stress on the other hand invariably results in a deterioration in performance and in the extreme, people panic and there is a breakdown in learning and a retrogression in skilled performance. Actions become confused. There is a lowering of attention and concentration. Reaction time lengthens with the competitor becoming much slower to react than normally. The problem is that under severe stress attention tends to become increasingly internally focused rather than task orientated. Competitors can start thinking about the social consequences of failure, about what spectators such as coaches and selectors might be thinking. Certainly, it is the case that attention can become focused on early mistakes so that the performer is failing to respond to the present situation and is failing to plan ahead. He worries about missed chances and about his 'bad luck'. Such self-preoccupation is characterized by doubts and feelings of inadequacy. Competitors sometimes start to engage in negative self-talk. Negative statements, which abound in junior tennis match tournaments include:

> 'I don't believe it'
> 'This is hopeless'
> 'You're so slow'
> 'I can't play on this "heap" (court)'
> 'What am I doing here?'

Obviously a competitor who engages in negative self-talk is not really concentrating on the match or on the task at hand. He/she is not really trying to work out how the match can be won.

The adverse influences of competitive stress affect people in different ways. In ball games the play of the anxious player is often rigid, inflexible, stereotyped and predictable. He is self preoccupied and overconcerned with his/her own performance. At junior level some youngsters are very tense and seem to become 'frozen' and 'rooted to the spot'. Under severe stress there can be a breakdown in learning and a return to a more primitive or earlier form of response or lower level of skill. In tennis, for example, this means that the skilled player may very well start pushing and patting the ball much as he had done when he had first begun to learn to play the game. There is, thus, a retrogression in skill and instances of this occurring under extreme stress at junior level are not unknown — the term 'hacking' is generally used to refer to this sort of play.

Some performers under the stress of competition can become very active but in an ineffective and unintelligent way. They report feelings of 'being rushed', of losing control of the situation. In tennis, for example, some players suddenly start to 'attack the net' on an extremely slow court which is an inappropriate and quite disastrous strategy. Unforced errors such as the double fault in tennis is another indication of the adverse effects of competitive stress.

Highly skilled players seldom serve double faults in practice and they simply should not do so in competition.

Tolerance for Stress

Tolerance for stress varies according to individual differences in personality, motivation, ability and experience. This means that what is a stressful situation for one competitor is not necessarily so for another. Reactions vary considerably. Thus in a sports context the presence of spectators has an inhibitory effect upon some players but enhances the performance of others. But not only are there differing reactions towards stress between individuals but there also are differences for the same individual who may overreact to stress in one situation but not in another. Even for the same activity the degree of stress for a person can vary from one occasion to another, which serves to indicate the intrinsic variability of personality. For some reason or other people can feel more confident on some days than on others for no readily identifiable reason.

The predisposition to react to stressful situations is closely related to levels of arousal. Research has concentrated upon two broad personality variations. These are the habitual, normal or chronic level of arousal on the one hand and the speed and extent to which arousal levels rise with the introduction of stress on the other. Thus introverted people who are generally more highly activated than extraverted individuals and neurotic individuals who are relatively easily aroused are particularly vulnerable to stressful conditions. On the other hand, extraverts with a normally lower level of arousal are less likely to become overactivated in competition than introverts. Indeed, extraverts tend to enjoy noise and crowds and actively to seek stimulation. They therefore tend to be at their best under these conditions. Nervous, tense individuals have a low tolerance for stress both physically and psychologically. On the other hand, stable, calm, temperamentally robust individuals can withstand greater degrees of stress and tend to perform better under stressful conditions than normally. It is for this reason that it is frequently argued that temperamental stability is a pre-condition for consistently successful performance at a high level.

Beginners and moderate performers have a relatively low tolerance for stress and this is blatantly apparent when an audience is present. Tolerance for stress is also influenced by past experience and in particular past experiences of similar situations which they are about to encounter. Experience of stress and the audience effect are discussed at some length in the following sections.

Experience of Stress

Much is made in sport of the value of experience for learning to cope with stressful competitive situations. It is frequently assumed that the positive benefits of experience in the reduction of stress will be automatic. As one manager of a junior sports training scheme used to be always saying 'Competition's the thing, competition's the thing'. There is clearly no doubt that repeated exposure to stress can enable an athlete to habituate to that stress, to become more familiar with it and thereby to learn how to cope with it more effectively. However, should the athlete's tolerance level be greatly exceeded then the experience will almost certainly be counterproductive and give rise to emotional problems, negative attitudes and loss of confidence. Nonetheless there is an almost compulsive obsession in some sports with the importance of continual competitive play to the neglect of other important considerations such as practice, the acquisition of skill and the emotional health of the individual. British tennis players go off on long overseas tours, for example, and in most cases fail to get beyond the qualifying rounds of the major tournaments for which they enter. However, despite abysmal results and the depressing effect on morale the notion persists that as the result of extensive tours players will become tough seasoned campaigners much in the same way as troops do in war or as at least some do.

But research by Eysenck and Rachman (1965) shows that experience does not always have the anticipated, desirable training effect. Indeed, the reverse can happen and it is well known that some soldiers during warfare experience neurotic breakdowns. Again Welford (1967), in studies of airline pilots, shows that prolonged experience of stress can lead to loss of efficiency and accident proneness leading to enforced early retirement.

In a sports context the differential effects of experience, stress reactions and performance have been studied by Fenz of the University of Waterloo in Canada. In his investigations (Fenz and Epstein, 1969; Fenz and Jones, 1972) of parachute jumpers or sky divers Fenz studied the stress reactions of novice and experienced performers. In this particular activity the stress of the situation is extreme since life itself is at risk. An interesting finding of these researchers was that not only were there differences in the stress responses of experienced and naïve jumpers as indicated by physiological measures of arousal but also that marked differences existed between experienced jumpers of high ability and experienced jumpers of low ability. It was found that the successful parachutists, although having elevated levels of arousal on the morning of the event, were able to reduce these to just above the normal resting state immediately prior to the jump. This is the level of arousal which is optimal for a high standard of performance for this highly demanding activity which requires intense concentration and the ability to remain calm and in control of the situation. In the case of parachutists it is clear that experience alone does not serve to improve performance. The position is further complicated by evidence from the academic field that the experience of poor test performance leads to rather higher levels of performance in subsequent tests by low anxious subjects but that the reverse if true for high anxious students whose performances become worse and worse following initial failure (Mandler and Sarason, 1952). Mandler and Sarason argue that high levels of anxiety evoke responses which are incompatible with successful performance such as feelings of inadequacy and helplessness and the worry about public censure. These findings have much the same implications in a sports context as they do in an academic one and underline the need for a highly individualistic approach when preparing young people for competition. However, although people are often very well prepared intellectually for academic examinations and physically for competitive events in sport, systematic psychological preparation in the affective domain remains virtually non-existent in both these areas. The traditional view is that emotional adjustment is something which will come with experience or you simply 'Don't have what it takes' and there is nothing much which can be done about it. This 'survival of the fittest' approach pervades the professional scene in a number of sports, for example. Such slogans as 'when the going gets tough, the tough get going' and 'defeat is worse than death'. 'You have to live with defeat', which appear on the walls of some changing rooms in the USA typify this approach. Again, to take another example from sport, there is the belief that continual competitive play guarantees effective performance and progress. The reverse often happens and what in fact is generated is a very high level of unnecessary stress which serves in the end to undermine even the performance of the temperamentally robust.

The national tennis training schemes which operate in this country provide a glaring example of the dubious value of the experience of an activity in the form of continuous competitive play. Progress in so many cases seems to 'plateau out' around the age of 16 or so and indeed some players even appear to get worse. From observation it seems that many junior players are far more confident and play far better in practice matches than they do in tournaments. There are numerous instances of players whose performance in match play continually fails to do justice to their ability, whose results appear to be almost incompatible with talent and promise. This suggests a low tolerance for stress.

The situation probably arises as a direct result of a training policy which exposes young people to prolonged and quite unnecessary stress. This is presumably in the fallacious belief that stress, in the form of continual competitive play, guarantees effective performance and progress. It must be emphasized at this point that tournament play provides an opportunity for the assessment of ability under stressful conditions; it is far from being the ideal vehicle for its development. Situations in which a player's self-esteem and prestige are continually at stake constitute severe stress. This will have disruptive effects on progress and can serve to undermine the confidence of even the temperamentally robust. The policy leads to players becoming far too anxious and apprehensive to play well.

The cumulative effects of severe stress manifest themselves at tournaments in the form of bad language and racquet throwing. Sometimes the outward physical signs of tension are manifest. Some players look pale and tense with visible trembling of the limbs in some cases; others remain 'frozen' and 'rooted to the spot' and appear to be emotionally 'burnt out'. Many clearly have lost all enjoyment for the game and but for parental loyalties would probably leave the tournament scene altogether. In fact a number of promising 12-year-olds by the age of 16 have already forsaken the game for less harrowing pursuits (Davies, 1981).

Spectators and Performance: The Audience Effect

A frequent source of stress for the competitor is the presence of an audience. The effect of spectators upon a player's performance is the concern of social facilitation research and has received extensive investigation. The findings show that many factors can be involved and that onlookers can have a dramatic effect upon standards typically achieved during unobserved practice sessions. Sometimes performance is enhanced, sometimes it deteriorates and sometimes there is little discernible difference. The presence of other people is itself arousing. Thus the general effect of a crowd of spectators is to raise arousal levels which tends to disrupt the performance of beginners and moderate competitors but to lead to higher levels of achievement in the case of the superior athlete.

The nature of the relationship between spectators and a player's performance is a complex one and is determined by the particular factors involved in any one games situation and the several ways in which they may combine and interact with each other. Two groups of factors can readily be identified: those which relate to the individual in terms of his experience, skill and personality and those which relate to the actual composition of the audience in terms of status, role, knowledge of the sport and importance as this is perceived by the performer.

The general effect of the presence of spectators is to raise the arousal levels of the participants. This means that there is the tendency for the performance of simple and well-learned tasks to be facilitated and that of difficult and slightly learned tasks to become disrupted: particularly is this so with anxious people. Zajonc (1965) argues that with elevated arousal levels the dominant response is emitted. Thus in the case of the unskilled person his/her performance is worse than when he/she is unobserved because it is the incorrect responses which will be facilitated. On the other hand, in the case of the skilled person, elevated arousal levels lead to enhanced performance because it is the correct responses which will be emitted since these are the dominant ones.

Generally speaking, the performance of stable, confident players tends to improve when watched by spectators and that of nervous, anxious players to decline. It is, in fact, perfectly possible for nervous people to be performing better on average than stable people when they are not being watched but for the position to be completely reversed when an audience is introduced with stable people now playing that much better and the nervous people that much worse.

Research shows that the effects of an audience on performance is also related to ability with superior players doing better when watched and mediocre or moderate players tending to do worse than when they are unobserved. It is clearly the case that superior players at international level are frequently inspired to do better in front of a large crowd and to actually revel in the atmosphere. It is as though they really need the excitement generated by an enthusiastic crowd to reach the supreme heights of play of which they are capable. Denis Compton, for example, the great England test cricketer of the immediate post-war era is reported as saying that he would not be interested in playing if only to be watched by 'two men and a dog'. And in tennis there are clearly a number of players who manifestly enjoy the experience of playing before a capacity crowd on the centre court at Wimbledon and greatly prefer this to the relative quiet of the outside courts.

The evidence from controlled research concerning the relationship between ability, performance and the presence of spectators is borne out by the author's own impressions of the play of junior competitors at tennis tournaments. At the delightful Manor Park Club at Malvern where the Worcestershire Open Championships are held there are two superb match courts behind and above which is a large bank which provides an excellent grandstand view for all the parents and friends. For the player below the situation very much resembles a stage at a theatre and their exposure to this somewhat intimidating situation is complete. Able and confident players enjoy the experience and delight in demonstrating their talents before what is often a knowledgeable and appreciative audience. In contrast, inferior players, sensitive of their shortcomings, generally prefer the relative obscurity of the 'outside' courts. Certainly when placed on these two 'match courts' they are often embarrassed, become inhibited and therefore play far worse then usually. In some extreme cases what skill a young player does have just about disintegrates under the stress of the occasion. This is particularly the case when the player is being watched by other players of much greater status and is in line with research predictions. Not infrequently the mediocre player in this sort of situation deliberately expedites the end of the game by his obvious lack of effort and disinterest. Win or lose, the overriding consideration is to get off the court and reach the sanctuary and relative obscurity of the pavilion.

Older, more experienced players, tend to be less adversely affected by audience stress. However, the author once witnessed the virtually complete disintegration, albeit temporarily, of a tennis player's game who was of average club standard. This player was being watched in *practice* by a highly critical individual of some standing in sport and in the end was missing the ball when dropped from his own hand! This is an isolated case but it does illustrate at the extreme the adverse effects which the presence of spectators can have on even the experienced player albeit of moderate ability.

It is the perceived role of the observer which seems to be the important factor. The work of Cottrell (1968), Haas and Roberts (1975), Martens and Landers (1972) and Green (1983) suggest that where the observers occupy a critical, evaluative, judgmental role then this is a situation which generates arousal and is a highly stressful situation for the young competitor anxious to be making his way in the sport. This is in contrast to the situation when the observer is seen as occupying a positive, supportive, coaching or teaching role. Any resulting constructive technical analysis and assessment will generally be welcomed by young participants.

The effect of the evaluative role of selectors is obvious to anyone who has attended the British Junior Grasscourt Championships which are played at Eastbourne each year. The mere sight of the national officials and selectors approaching the courts is sufficient for some players to begin to appear uncertain and apprehensive. The author had first-hand experience of the evaluative audience effect when conducting a series of perceptual motor skill tests in schools. Upon the appearance of the headmaster, sometimes accompanied by a visiting inspector of schools, there were quite sharp changes in performance with some boys now performing far better and others far worse. It seems likely, therefore, that the more acute the stress, the more dramatic is the change in performance. At the extreme the stress generated by an evaluative audience becomes so overwhelming that in the words of Ziegler (1978) the athlete becomes a spectator of his/her own performance.

The term coaction denotes situations in which a number of individuals are engaged in the same activity at the same time. Sport is full of coactive situations such as occur in athletics, swimming, gymnastics and so forth. As with the presence of an audience the general effect of coaction is to raise arousal levels. This means that individuals who are optimally aroused for an event may well become over-aroused when joined by other competitors to the inevitable detriment in performance. As might be expected the larger the number of people engaged and the closer the proximity then the greater are the coaction effects and thus higher levels of arousal will frequently be generated.

For the majority of young players who are engaged in competitive activities, there will always be an audience whether people are actually physically present at the event or not. This 'hidden' audience will be the people who will be studying the results in the newspapers, namely the selectors, organizers, coaches and parents. The stress factor is operating here in this situation also for it is largely on the basis of the results that future teams and training squads will be selected. Young people are also frequently concerned not to let people down such as their coaches and parents. Thus the hidden audience is a source of worry which can serve to distract attention from the task at hand.

The Management of Competitive Stress

Introduction

Competitive stress can be managed. Strategies and techniques are available which enable performers in such highly demanding activities as sky-diving, springboard diving and Olympic gymnastics to control arousal levels and to reduce these immediately prior to competition. In this way people are able to remain calm, to make accurate judgments and generally to remain in control of situations.

Stress problems of sportmen and their reactions to them are highly individualistic. Each sportsperson is virtually unique and therefore competitors simply cannot be helped all in the same way.

However, although a highly individualistic approach is frequently required, certain established, basic strategies and techniques can be identified which are generally employed to varying degrees in the management of stress in sport. It is, of course, preferable to avoid exceeding a person's stress tolerance level. This is not always easy although it does happen that young people are sometimes exposed to quite unnecessarily stressful situations for which they are not adequately prepared emotionally. Such situations are best avoided. The problem is that people can become *conditioned* to experiencing stress reactions to the detriment of performance. They may have *learned* to become anxious and apprehensive. Further, in many instances, people become convinced that this will always be the case, that they will always experience discomforting feelings of anxiety in competitive situations. Not surprisingly, some people learn to dislike them, to hate them and refuse to take any further part despite their considerable potential ability. It is, therefore, incumbent on the coach or whoever is responsible for a young player's competitive match programme that he is not exposed to situations which greatly exceed his stress tolerance level. It is important that young players should gradually become acclimatized to the stressful situations which they will later encounter. 'Throw him in at the deep end' is just one of the myths which abound in competitive sport. It is a foolish policy and can have a disastrous effect on the confidence and competitive performance of young players. It is vital, therefore, for a young player's morale that tournament participation should be generally appropriate to a player's ability and temperament. Almost certainly where a player is feeling too anxious he will fail to do justice to his ability in the competitive match situation.

Strategies and Techniques

In the first instance it is helpful for competitors to be acquainted with the sources of stress and the general physiological, emotional, behavioural and cognitive reactions to stress. This is the educative phase and serves to give people greater self-awareness and thus an appreciation of the purpose and functions of the strategies employed in the management of stress.

Self-awareness means that people should readily learn to recognize the difference between a state of tension and a state of relaxation. Further, they should be able to recognize symptoms which predict the onset of tension and result in stress reactions. This means that they can initiate prompt counter alleviating measures. International athletes, for example, sometimes engage in relaxation exercises to reduce tension in the sports arena immediately prior to the race. Early awareness of the onset of tension is important because preliminary emotional reactions to stress 'trigger off' bodily feelings and sensations which adversely affect concentration and these bodily reactions serve further to heighten feelings of anxiety. What so often happens is that the individual becomes trapped, caught in a downward spiral of his own making. Reactions to stress become self-perpetuating and anxiety starts as the saying goes to 'feed on itself'.

Relaxation

The stress-prone competitor must learn to relax for a state of relaxation is quite incompatible with feelings of tension, worry and anxiety. Relaxation is a state of controlled and relatively stable level of arousal which is lower than that of the normal waking state. The competitor worries less in the relaxed state and his attention is not distracted by uncomfortable sensations which arise from excessive muscular tension. Progressive relaxation is a relaxation technique which has been widely found to be most effective in the reduction of stress. Progressive muscle relaxation was originally developed by Edmund Jacobson in the early 1930s. Jacobson's technique involved systematic tension followed by relaxation of all the major muscle groups in the body. Tensing a muscle really hard will produce a high level of relaxation in the muscle when it is subsequently relaxed. With regular practice on a daily basis over a period of several weeks, it becomes possible to relax within seconds. The aim should be for the state of relaxation to become the dominant response in competitive situations with a person sensing that he is becoming increasingly in control of his feelings. In the world of competitive sport relaxation is increasingly becoming to be recognized as an essential part of the preparation programme of the athlete as he faces the testing demands of competition at international level. Many athletes use self-induced relaxation (SIR) to reduce arousal levels to the optimum prior to their match or event. SIR can, in time, be practised on quite an incidental basis at odd moments during the day. Sessions can be for ten minutes duration or even as short as ten seconds. The benefits of acquiring the relaxation response are considerable and these are detailed in the following section.

Progressive relaxation

Progressive relaxation is a highly effective technique employed extensively in the management of stress, tension, anxiety and worry. An excessively high level of arousal frequently gives rise to feelings of doubt and induced negative thinking. On the other hand, in the relaxed state, motor coordination is better, as is concentration since attention is not distracted by uncomfortable bodily sensations, such as 'butterflies' in the stomach arising from excessive muscular tension. Accordingly performance is frequently enhanced. Relaxation serves to inhibit panic reactions such as indecision and undue hesitancy and enables the competitor to be decisive, calm and controlled in tense situations which are occurring all the time in sport such as match points in tennis, vital penalty kicks in soccer and championship deciding putts in golf. Progressive relaxation delays fatigue and leads to better sleep. Thus the benefits of acquiring the relaxation response are considerable in terms not only of performance but also with respect to the emotional health of the young sportsman which is often placed at risk when participating in highly competitive individual sports. The pressures can be considerable and are evident even to the casual observer. At the breakfast tables at the hotels and boarding houses of Eastbourne, for example, when the British National Junior Tennis Championships take place, appetites have virtually disappeared.

Progressive relaxation should be practised in conjunction with other stress-management techniques. The programme which is outlined below in this chapter is a modification of Jacobson's programme (Jacobson, 1938). Regular practise on a daily basis is important. The aim should be to practise progressive relaxation to the point where it becomes a well-learned response. For the anxious player, the aim should be for relaxation to become the dominant response in stress situations such as competitive matches.

Relaxation Programme

Make yourself comfortable in an easy chair. Close your eyes and go as limp as you can, let the weight in your body go completely, let your arms and legs feel heavy, like sand bags. Relax completely, start to breathe deeply and slowly, deeply and slowly, deeply and slowly. Become consciously aware of the rhythmic pattern of your breathing, thinking only of this as you breathe deeply and slowly, deeply and slowly. Continue for five minutes or so until you feel refreshed.

People are often unaware of the physical tension in themselves. You can achieve greater awareness of the tension in your body by alternately tensing and relaxing various muscles. Beginning with the right hand clench it very hard for a few seconds and then relax. Repeat again, clenching the hand, holding the tension and then relaxing. Now clench your right hand again but this time not so hard, feeling the difference in the lower tension level before relaxing again. Now with the palm of your right hand facing downwards, stretch your fingers outwards and upwards. Feel the tension and then relax. Repeat the procedure again, stretching the fingers for a few moments before relaxing. Stretch your fingers outwards and upwards again, but this time not as far so that you feel that the tension is less. Do these exercises now with your left hand, clenching, stretching, holding for a few seconds and then relaxing. You should next proceed in turn to alternately tensing and relaxing the muscles in your forearms, upper arms and shoulders, your neck and facial muscles in your forearms, upper arms and shoulders, your neck and facial muscles, your forehead, your calf and thigh muscles and now your feet and toes. Try twisting your feet inwards and outwards. Next start to move your feet and toes upwards and back towards you, at the same time depressing your legs downwards. Finally turn to tensing the muscles in your stomach, chest and back.

You should now conclude your relaxation programme by spending a little time concentrating on tensing your whole body, holding the tension for a few seconds and then relaxing. Finally you can further deepen the level of relaxation by taking a deep breath on concluding the exercises. Doing these exercises will help you to recognize and to sense the physical tension in various parts of your body and the extent to which you can become really physically relaxed and more mentally at ease.

You will need to practise these exercises over and over again until you can relax at will and have control over the physical tension in your body. Some of the exercises can be done at odd times during the day, as when waiting for a bus or train or standing in some queue for example. Try whenever possible to use some of these exercises in situations which are stressful for you. You will need to persevere with them over a period of some weeks or maybe months, particularly if you are a rather anxious person. But they do work and are quite pleasant to perform. Practise the exercises every day and note the gradual improvement in your ability to reduce tension as you progress to the stage where you are a much more relaxed person generally. With extensive practice it becomes possible to relax within seconds.

Biofeedback training

Biofeedback training can be employed as a useful facilitating procedure for training in relaxation. Important information can be acquired using biofeedback procedures concerning the physiological functioning of the body including arousal levels. The use of biofeedback measures speeds up the process of acquiring the relaxation response by providing the individual with *objective* knowledge of his progress. In the absence of sophisticated electronic equipment, a common procedure is to measure fingertip temperature; another is to measure heart rate. Either heart rate or fingertip temperature must be taken before and after relaxation sessions. Heart rate can be measured by counting beats for ten seconds and then simply multiplying by six to fix the rate per minute. With respect to fingertip temperature, this should begin to show a rise after relaxation sessions. This is because in the more relaxed state fingertip temperature rises because the flow of blood to the extremities of the body is facilitated. The importance of the use of these measures is that they provide an individual with 'feedback' which provides objective evidence of his/her progress. Fingertip temperature, for example, provides precise objective and visual information of the progress which an individual is making towards acquiring this skill. Thus, people do not have to rely on their own subjective feelings as to whether they are learning to relax, for example. Objective evidence in terms of biofeedback measures means that people are able to relate what they do in terms of practice to what happens as the result of such practice. Thus biofeedback procedures apart from their highly motivating value in terms of objective knowledge of progress provide the individual with *information*. This means that he is able to adjust his training programme in the light of the information he has received. On a trial and test basis, therefore, the individual is able to assess, for example, whether more practice is needed generally or just with certain muscle groups to achieve the best results. He is therefore able to determine the optimal lengths and frequency of the practice sessions. For fingertip temperature all that is needed is an inexpensive hand thermometer although a more expensive digital thermometer will record even the slightest changes.

The importance of feedback for skill acquisition was emphasized in chapter 2. Biofeedback training facilitates the acquisition of the relaxation response providing the learner with diagnostic information and with knowledge of his progress. The biofeedback training procedure has demonstrated that it is possible to have voluntary control over such bodily functions as blood pressure and heart rate, which at one time was not considered possible.

Learning to accommodate to stress
Continued exposure to moderate or gradually increasing degrees of stress provides the opportunity for people to adjust to competitive stress and to learn how to handle it. The pressures in practice matches and activities can be built up in all sorts of ways by the ingenious coach. Practice matches provide an effective means of developing the emotional capacities of the sports competitor. The types of stresses experienced in tournaments and matches can be simulated in practice conditions. The idea is to simulate, but in a gradual manner, the types of stresses in practice which the competitor himself *says* he experiences in competition and to get nearer and nearer to the competitive match situation. Practice games can be played as matches, employing some kind of incentive. This might take the form of buying the drinks afterwards or whatever can be mutually agreed between the players to increase the importance of the game, provided it doesn't cause friction but gives a certain 'edge' to the practice. By increasing the incentive you, of course, increase the stress. This can be done providing the tolerance level is not greatly exceeded. Learning to accommodate, to cope with gradually increasing degrees of stress is sound psychological practice and will improve the player's capacity to withstand the pressures of competitive tournament play. Simulated conditions in practice to an actual game situation can be arranged even without a partner. Players can imagine, for example, that they are serving with the score at 0-40, 15-40 or whatever. They should try keeping relaxed and concentrating in these conditions of practice so that they will then transfer to an actual tournament situation which, sooner or later, they will meet unless they have a cannon-ball serve with which they never miss!

Adequate emotional preparation is seen as being important if the sportsperson is to be able to cope with competitive stress and if he/she is to remain in control of situations. The various strategies and techniques which are available to the coach are explored in detail in chapter 6 which is entirely concerned with the psychological preparation of the sportsperson for competitive events.

Intrinsic motivation

An important strategy for the coach to follow in the management of stress is the enhancement of intrinsic motivation. The principal interest of the intrinsically motivated sportsperson is in the sport rather than in social considerations such as financial reward and social recognition and approval. With social considerations assuming secondary importance sportspeople can become less concerned about 'letting people down' and about what others might say or think. These social considerations are a potent source of stress (Davies, 1986). Setting clearly defined objective goals on a weekly basis facilitates intrinsic motivation. Intrinsically motivated sportspeople are obviously in a better position to withstand frustrations and temporary setbacks. Following a reverse, they become mainly concerned in analysing their performance and how it is to be improved. This is the kind of positive approach which players should constantly be seeking to develop.

Preparation

The adverse, disruptive effects of competitive stress will be minimal when the individual is thoroughly prepared for a contest both physically, mentally and emotionally and has a complete mastery of the skill. Thus in tennis, for example, court strategies must be repeated over and over again until they become virtually automatic. The same consideration applies to a player's stroke repertoire. The strokes which will be vulnerable under the stress of competition will be those which have been recently acquired and which have been insufficiently practised. These invariably will be the first to break down when a player becomes too tense and starts to lose self-confidence. Thus players may start to 'run round their backhand' for example and to abandon their first service and start serving second services in service games. Thorough preparation therefore is essential if the sportsman is to cope with the rigours of competitive stress. It is not necessarily the best player who wins but the player who is best prepared.

Devaluing the importance of the event

An extremely effective strategy to employ in some cases is to devalue the importance of the match! There are some obvious difficulties with this approach. Coaches and managers are likely to become alarmed if not outraged at the thought that it might be in the best interests of some of their players if they were not to try so hard! Indeed managers of football clubs are convinced that it is effort or to use the jargon of the game 'get stuck in' which decides whether their team wins or loses. However, emphasizing the importance of the event increases the stress and dressing rooms can become centres of apprehension and fear. But for players who are doing well in the practice matches but badly in the competitive ones then it might well be that in this latter situation they become over-aroused and experience adverse stress reactions to the detriment of their performance. Simple, elementary errors occur through poor motor-control and a loss of concentration with players sometimes being reduced to a state of panic. Thus the missing of simple goals typify the promotional and relegation matches in the football league at the end of each season. Such mistakes simply never occur in practice games. Thus one explanation for this situation is that competitors become too highly motivated, worried and anxious. One of the major differences between the practice match and the actual match is one of importance. Thus reducing the importance of the event serves to limit the stress reactions and therefore the performance of the anxious over-aroused competitor will accordingly improve. In some cases, therefore, it can be beneficial to reduce excessive drive, to calm people, to 'psych players down' rather than 'up' or perhaps, more accurately, '*out*'. Research indicates that competitive performance can be improved by strategies which serve to reduce excessive drive and paradoxically though it may seem one of these is to devalue the importance of the contest which no doubt will be a difficult strategy to implement, particularly with respect to football managers who are obsessed with commitment — they will need some convincing. It should be emphasized, however, that strategies designed to reduce excessive drive should only be employed in the case of the highly motivated and highly aroused and anxious sportsperson. For people who are not particularly anxious or overconcerned such a strategy is obviously not appropriate. In this case competitors will need to be 'psyched up' employing such techniques as mental preparation, the cultivation of positive attitudes and use of imagery.

Modelling behaviour
Highly anxious people benefit when they have the opportunity to observe a person coping successfully in highly stressful competitive situations. Modelling of performance characteristics such as stroke play is, of course, not uncommon in sport and is popularly recognized. However, what is perhaps not so well appreciated is that modelling of behaviour can also be helpful in terms of learning to cope with stress. Observing a sportsman performing well under stress in a positive way

provides an observer with a model to copy and to imitate for his/her own future behaviour in similar competitive situations. As it is anxious people are particularly responsive to modelling strategies. It has also been found that anxious people benefit from just listening to successful performers relate how they are able to cope with competitive pressures and the methods which they adopt (Sarason, 1975). Anxious people are generally receptive to suggestion and are thus enabled to adopt their behaviour successfully in future for the enhancement of their performance.

Cognitive modification
Competitively anxious people tend to become self-preoccupied. Concentration is frequently poor because the anxious person worries and does not attend to the task at hand such as performing well in the game or contest. However, such behaviour can be modified by following certain coping procedures aimed at countering self-preoccupation (Sarason, 1972). Cognitive modification involves cognitive reappraisal and it is important, therefore, that the competitor learns to reappraise competitive situations in a positive way. It is a question of shifting the focus of attention from irrelevant thinking to task-orientated behaviour and to eliminate worry. The purpose is to develop a positive attitude and a constructive approach to situations. Negative attitudes solve nothing. They mitigate against successful performance since both concentration and confidence are inevitably adversely affected. Indications of a negative approach occur when players start to blame the conditions such as the weather, the playing surface and their equipment and to complain about 'having no luck' and about nothing being right. With a positive approach, on the other hand, an attempt is being made to solve the problem, to cope with the conditions. Competitively anxious people do tend to have negative attitudes and to engage in a lot of negative self-talk during the actual event. Some examples frequently heard include:

> 'This is hopeless'
> 'What luck'
> 'What weather'
> 'What a ground'
> 'I can never play well here'

Such statements are indicative of the fact that the competitor is not really concentrating and that he is not really trying to work out how he/she can improve his/her performance and win.

With a positive approach on the other hand, the competitor is working for a solution to the problem, whilst being fully aware of the difficulties. He/she persists and does not give up in the face of initial difficulty. He/she is continually involved with trying to find a solution to the problem. If one approach fails then another is tried, then another, if this becomes necessary. In tennis, for example, racquet and ball abuse solve nothing and are indicative of a player's negative attitude and approach. With a positive approach in this activity the competitor will be seeking weaknesses in his opponent's game and trying to exploit these. Cognitive modification, therefore, emphasizes the importance of developing and maintaining a constructive mood and approach. This is an effective means of coping with distractions, worries and self-preoccupations which give rise to tension and stress. Positive self-talk helps, while negative self-statements do not and must be eliminated. Positive statements such as 'This one's going in, I'll attack his/her backhand' serve to direct a competitor's attention to the task before him and thus to improve concentration. Repeated use of positive statements will encourage a competitor to start thinking positively and to acquire positive concepts.

A practical start can be made by drawing up a list of positive statements which can be used both before and during a game to replace the negative ones. Saying such things as: 'That's my fourth ace today', 'Now, I'm beginning to hit some really good shots'; 'My mental preparation is really beginning to pay off' and so on. In this way the player's attention becomes more focused on the game itself and he/she is less likely to be disturbed by factors which adversely affect concentration such as the noise of spectators, bad bounces, inaccurate line calls and so forth. Preliminary diagnosis is important since it does help to make people aware of behaviour which is counterproductive.

In cases where competitors are playing markedly better in practice than they are in competition, it might help to try to adopt the same attitude, the same feelings, the same mental approach towards a competitive game that they have towards a practice one. If players enjoy the game and play well in practice then they should try to enjoy competitive events as much. Here again a positive approach, the use of positive statements will help to achieve this state of mind. Ideally competitive events should be viewed as a learning experience, as an opportunity to acquire a positive attitude, to develop concentration and thus to enhance performance. Unfortunately most players and their coaches are consumed with the results and wins or losses are regarded as the sole criteria of the value of matches. It is a superficial naïve approach to the acquisition of skill in sport.

A positive approach can also be developed and maintained by

keeping in mind images and experiences of successful past performances in competition. It is important to set aside so much time each day to practise these techniques — an actual specific length of time should be set aside for this and recorded.

It might be considered that people who look at competitive situations in a positive way are really only engaging in wishful thinking. This is certainly not the correct interpretation of the strategy, which is now being advanced. With a positive approach, the competitor is trying to improve upon his performance whilst being fully alive to the difficulties. He/she is trying to do something about the situation rather than just doing nothing at all.

Cognitive modification, therefore, is principally concerned with the worry which arises from competitive stress. Diagnosis and assessment of a sportsman's negative thoughts during competition is important. Competitive situations will need to be reappraised and viewed in a more constructive way. One way is to view competitive events as important learning experiences from which the player stands to gain in terms of future performance.

Systematic desensitization procedures
The systematic desensitization procedure is a most effective technique employed in the management of stress over a wide range of performance situations including sport. It is used, for example, to help people cope with stage fright and to overcome anxiety, apprehension and loss of confidence following injury. This occurs in the case of rugby full-backs, wicket-keepers, batsmen and goalkeepers to give but a few examples. Thus in these cases where the set back has been quite severe, the basic relaxation programme may not in itself be sufficient.

To illustrate the procedure, we can take a hypothetical case of a goalkeeper who has lost confidence in his ability to catch high centres in the penalty area and particularly with respect to corner kicks. The problem is not an uncommon one with goalkeepers whose position in the side is a rigorously demanding one and any errors can be calamitous for the team. One first division goalkeeper, for example, known to the author, used frequently to remark that 'I just long for 4.45pm to come on a Saturday afternoon'. Others have had nervous breakdowns resulting in early retirement from the game.

Desensitizing Procedure

The first step is to draw up a list or a hierarchy of anxiety-provoking stimuli which are directly related to the fear situation. With the aid of a counsellor, coach or sports psychologist, the goalkeeper identifies say fifteen situations related to his experiences of goalkeeping.

These items are then drawn up into a list (Table 5) with number 15 being the item which causes least anxiety and the remaining items being listed in turn as they elicit increasing degrees of anxiety culminating in item number 1, which is the match itself.

TABLE 5:

Hierarchical list of stress-provoking stimuli (hypothetical case of a goalkeeper)

1	Playing the actual match
2	Full-scale 'friendly' match amongst players of own club
3	Corner kick with 14 players massed in penalty area
4	Corner kick with 11 players 8 inside penalty area 4 on goal-line
5	Corner kick with 11 players 6 inside penalty area 3 on goal-line
6	Corner kick with 11 players 5 inside penalty area 2 on goal-line
7	Corner kick with 11 players 4 inside penalty area 1 on goal-line
8	Corner kick with 11 players 3 inside penalty area
9	Corner kick with 6 players 2 inside penalty area
10	Corner kick with 5 players 1 inside penalty area
11	Corner kick with 4 players outside penalty area
12	Corner kick with 3 players outside penalty area
13	Corner kick with 2 players outside penalty area
14	Corner kick with 1 player outside penalty area
15	Corner kick with kicker only on the field

Having drawn up the agreed list of stress situations, the next step in the procedure is to achieve a deep state of relaxation. The relaxation technique generally employed with sportsmen is that of progressive relaxation (Jacobson, 1938). In this relaxed state as vivid image, as possible, is obtained of each item beginning with item 15, the situation causing the least anxiety.

Imagery or visualization needs practice but it is a technique widely used in the mental preparation of sportspeople for competition. The idea is to get as vivid an image as possible of each situation using an internal focus. Using an internal focus, the sportsperson is actively engaged in the activity in a mental sense. He/she is not a spectator in the exercise as if he/she were watching him/herself on film or using an external focus.

With the internal focus, the sportsperson visualizes him/herself actually performing, actually doing the activity. In the case of the example in table 5, the goalkeeper would see the corner kick being taken and the ball in flight as though it were actually happening and he/she is there in the action and taking appropriate action. In other words, his/her role is very much an active one to the extent that recordings can be made of actual muscle movements. Visualization is a skill and consequently needs practice. But with systematic practice it becomes possible to have vivid and controlled images of situations. Apart from eliminating feelings of anxiety, relaxation is important because in the relaxed state the ability to visualize performance situations is facilitated.

In the case of the goalkeeper, the hierarchical list could be extended if necessary. At item 14, for example, the additional player on the field to the player taking the corner kick would be imagined say 10 feet from the goal then say 7, then 4 feet from the goal line, then 3, and then 2 for example.

All the evidence concerning systematic desensitization points to the fact that should an individual reach item 1, where, in the case of the goalkeeper, he can imagine playing a full scale match without feeling unduly nervous, the chances are that this will also prove to be the case in the actual match. A vivid controlled image is important. Imaging is a skill which can be acquired by systematic sustained and guided practice. Images of stress situations and the subjective feelings of nervousness which they elicit are paralleled by heightened arousal levels as measured by heart rate, respiration rate and skin conductance. Systematic desensitization is a most effective technique in the management of stress-related problems and in particular in the case of 'stage fright'. Table 6 gives, by way of illustration, a hypothetical case of a tennis player facing the prospect of a match on the Centre Court at Wimbledon for the first time. 'Stage fright', of course, is not uncommon among young sportspeople who are suddenly thrust into the spotlight of a large public arena and the searching critical attention of the media. A desensitization programme can be quite short. As few as eight one-hour sessions can bring about a dramatic improvement as Tryon (1980) has shown from her research in the academic field with nervous university examinees.

In the case of both relaxation and desensitization techniques, the use of audio cassette tape programmes has been found to be an effective medium of instruction.

The important point about visualizing situations which evoke anxiety in competitive sports situations is that this medium can be almost as effective as the real-life experience. In practical terms visualization has a number of advantages. Situations can be tailored to

TABLE 6:
Hierarchical list of stress-provoking stimuli
Stage fright: Centre Court match, Wimbledon

1	Starting the match
2	Walking on court
3	Listening to the announcement of the match
4	Waiting in the dressing room
5	Changing in the dressing room
6	Glimpsing the opponent
7	Entering the ground
8	Morning of the match — getting ready to travel
9	The night before the match — lying in bed thinking
10	The evening before the match at the ground

meet the particular needs of the competitor and it is, of course, economical both in terms of time and resources. As we have said earlier, repeated experience of a stress provoking situation does not necessarily solve anything. Indeed it can make things even worse. All the evidence concerning flying, making public speeches, taking examinations shows that anxiety is not necessarily allayed. Indeed, if the experience is unpleasant, such as a series of humiliating defeats, it is likely to make things very much worse. A more sophisticated research orientated approach is needed. Thus the central strategy to use in extreme fear provoking situations is to pair these in visualization sessions with a state of relaxation. Relaxation is incompatible with anxiety. Thus using relaxation with the visualization of the situation, which elicits anxiety, the sportsperson begins to learn a new association. If the relaxation response is dominant, no anxiety should be experienced. The point being made is that since anxiety reactions to stressful situations in sport are learned then they can, therefore, equally well be unlearned with practice using specific strategies and techniques which have been referred to in this chapter.

A consistent finding in research is that anxiety levels are at their highest immediately before the competitive event is due to begin (Figure 4). It seems that thinking about the stressful event to come affects some people to quite a considerable degree. They become nervous and apprehensive and, if possible, sometimes avoid going to the ground until the last moment. However, once the match or event gets under way anxiety levels begin to fall. They fall generally, presumably because competitors become involved in the action and the 'waiting is over'. The rate and extent to which anxiety levels fall, however, varies with the sport. The greater the expenditure of physical energy the quicker anxiety is dissipated. Thus, with physically demanding activities such as boxing, rowing, middle distance running, anxiety levels fall relatively sharply whereas, in contrast, high jumping, archery, goalkeeping and golf with relatively little energy being expended competitors can sometimes remain tense and anxious throughout the contest. This could well be the reason why sportsmen engaging in these activities do occasionally suffer from serious loss of form. Golfers, for example, even of international standing, have been known to suffer from attacks of the 'yips' when putting which resulted in their temporary and occasionally permanent absence from the world class game.

Figure 4: Anxiety/arousal levels prior to and during competition

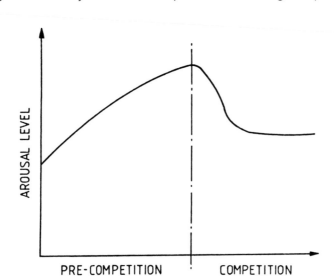

Mild fatigue can help to reduce nervousness. Thus anxious players might benefit by undertaking some fairly vigorous exercise prior to a competitive game. This will serve to reduce physical tension and enable them to feel more relaxed.

Conclusion

This chapter has been largely concerned with the sources, nature and management of competitive stress in sport. The various bodily, emotional and behavioural reactions to stress as they affect people have been discussed. And the various relationships which exist between stress and performance in a competitive sports context have been examined. From this, it will be apparent that reactions to stress are highly individualistic and that each sportsperson is virtually unique. Thus it is evident, sportspeople with stress problems simply cannot be helped all in the same way. This means that diagnosis of the problems and an assessment of the individual needs of the sportsperson is imperative for help to be effective.

What we have argued in this chapter is that competitive stress can be managed. Several techniques and strategies are available which have been found to be effective in the treatment of sportspeople with stress-related problems. There is no need to resort to drugs. Sportspeople can be helped and can help themselves to the extent that they are able to do justice to their ability and commitment in the competitive sports situation.

Anxiety is often a critical factor influencing successful performance in competitive sport. Indeed, stability of temperament is a necessary prerequisite for performance at a consistently high level. However, it remains the case that much undue competitive stress is unnecessary and is clearly avoidable.

Young sportspeople, for example, should not be put under undue pressure from over-ambitious single-minded parents and coaches where they are viewed almost as pocket adults. They should not be exposed to competitive situations for which they are not sufficiently emotionally mature nor adequately prepared.

Competitive stress can frequently be reduced by tackling one of its major sources which is uncertainty. The way to do this is by providing the young sportsperson with as much information as is possible. Knowledge of progress, of areas to be developed, are important and particularly is this so where no accurate objective yardstick exists, which is the case in competitive games where wins and losses are not necessarily an accurate assessment of potential achievement. The sportsperson needs to have information, for example, about the competitive conditions, about the opposition and about what is expected of him/her. Mutually agreed short-term goals need to be worked out between the sportsperson and his/her coach, which will provide knowledge of progress. Classified goals help to clear uncertainty. There is rapport with the coach resulting in increased self-confidence.

Competitive stress can also be reduced by tackling a further major source which frequently occurs and this is a quite exaggerated importance of a particular event or match. In cases where people become extremely anxious about a forthcoming competition then it might well be that they are viewing it out of all proportion to its actual importance. They need to put the competition in its proper perspective. Any match is of less importance than a serious injury or illness for example. Successful performance in competition is not the be-all and end-all. In any case a particular competitive event needs to be seen as just one in a programme of matches which provide the competitor with a learning opportunity in such important concerns as attitude, persistence, concentration and emotional control. Viewed as a learning experience, from which to gain important insights for future development, matches will accordingly lose much of their stress since they are now probably being viewed from a totally different perspective than is generally the case, which is simply to equate losses with failure and wins with success and to leave it at that. This is a serious shortcoming in the development of any young player which is to a large extent dependent on the quality of the analysis which should be undertaken by the coach following competitive matches. We shall return to this question in chapter 6 which is concerned with the psychological preparation and development of the sportsperson.

The salient point, which it is hoped will have emerged from this chapter, is that the ability to perform well under pressure is a skill and is therefore learned. It is learned by appropriate sustained practice using a variety of strategies and techniques which have been reviewed in this chapter. Last minute, off-the-cuff advice and unrehearsed self-instruction is likely to be of little value. What is needed is the mastery of effective techniques which enable the individual to remain calm, decisive and in control of highly stressful situations which prevail in competitive sport. The 1987 Wimbledon Championships provided a reminder that even the best players in the world can be vulnerable to the pressures of competitive stress. Ivan Lendl, the world's number 1 player, double-faulted against Pat Cash at crucial moments of the Men's Final. He had previously done the same against Jimmy Connors in the USA Championships. A double fault is an unforced error, since the opponent is not involved. The highly skilled performer should simply not serve double-faults. When he/she does so, it is a likely indication of the breakdown of skilled performance under competitive stress. And as John Barrett, the BBC commentator said at the time, the match would be won or lost in the mind!

The management of competitive stress embraces the following central objectives:

1   The ability to control voluntarily arousal or activation levels of the nervous system.

2   The ability to focus the attention on the requirements of the match situation and to shut out self-preoccupied internal worrying behaviour.

3   The acquisition of a constructive mood and a positive approach. This means looking to overcome temporary frustration and initial difficulty.

4   The ability to perform consistently well under pressure.

Chapter 5

Anticipation in Ball Games

Introduction

Contrary to popular belief anticipation is something which is learned. It is not something which is natural and which some people are lucky to have and others not. All players, including the champions have to learn to anticipate. Some learn faster than others and some have greater capacities for learning than others but, nonetheless, anticipation is something which every games player must master if he/she is to improve. The ways in which anticipation is learned are outlined.

Anticipation is one of the really important keys to success in all ball games and certainly to become a top-ranking tennis player, for example, a lot of time must be devoted to improving the speed of anticipation. Towards the end of this chapter ways in which anticipation can be significantly improved are outlined. But first it is important to look at some of the facts concerning anticipation and how it is that the top players are able to react as fast as they do.

Exceptionally good anticipation is the hallmark of the champion. All the really great players have excellent anticipation to the extent that to the spectators it is almost uncanny. The crowds at Wimbledon, for example, are constantly being amazed at the way some passing shots are picked up by the volleyer and the speed of reaction when all four players are rallying at the net in doubles. It is because the champion performer anticipates correctly that he/she appears to be unhurried and to have so much more time to play his/her shots than the average player.

Contrary to popular belief, anticipation is something which is learned. It is not something which is natural and which some people are lucky to have and others not. All players, including the champions, have to learn to anticipate. Some learn faster than others and some have greater capacities for learning than others but, nonetheless, anticipation is something which every tennis player must master if he/she is to improve.

So how is anticipation learned and how are reactions speeded up? Let us take a look at strokes in tennis. In the production of any tennis stroke there is a sequence of sub-routines or parts which go to make up the complete stroke. These form the incoming visual signals which the receiver must perceive or 'read' if he/she is to predict just where the ball will go, whether across the court, down the sideline or high to the baseline, for example. Some of the actions of a player as he/she prepares to make a shot will give information about his/her intentions but others will not and being irrelevant must be ignored. The highly skilled player identifies the significant actions or cues as they are generally called relatively early in the sequence and ignores the irrelevant cues. The moderate player, on the other hand, may have difficulty in selecting relevant cues from irrelevant cues or he/she may only identify them relatively late in the sequence, perhaps too late to initiate any effective action. Thus we find at the public park level that the game is sprinkled with frequent seemingly convulsive stab-like shots at the ball because the players fail to anticipate. Indeed, they often begin to react after the ball has been hit which means that they have insufficient time to produce a reasonably controlled shot. This situation arises because the players are not focusing their attention on the opponent's movements or, if they are, then they don't really know what to be looking for. Their anticipation is poor because their concentration is poor.

The popular notion of concentration among the vast majority of club players seems to be limited to watching the ball! When coaches and players are asked what is meant by concentration the invariable reply is to 'watch the ball'. Indeed, young players are told this over and over again in training and when a mistake is made then players will sometimes remind themselves out loud to 'watch the ball'. But to perform at the highest levels concentration has to be much, very much more than this in order to anticipate and return the ball effectively.

The speed at which a player anticipates is of vital importance if he/she is going to get anywhere in ball games. This is because the speed of the ball is sometimes such that it is extremely doubtful whether it is possible to predict ball flight from the ball itself. In other words, if you do not anticipate sufficiently early you will not be able to cope physically with some returns. It has been estimated for example, that a ball can be travelling at speeds in excess of 100 mph. Pancho Gonzales' service was timed at 120mph and that of Roscoe Tanner at even higher speeds. And in baseball it has been calculated that the ball can be travelling so fast that a player would have to initiate his swing when the ball is some twenty-five feet away. Thus the speed at which the ball frequently travels, together with the interval which occurs between the point in time at which the ball is struck by the opponent and the need to initiate a response, explains why anticipation is such a crucial factor in many racquet games other than tennis.

As has been said earlier, champion performers are characterized by having exceptionally good anticipation and this is something which has to be learned. The manner in which this happens involves experience and practice of the right kind. As a result of his experience of playing tennis against hundreds of good players the highly skilled performer builds up a vast fund of knowledge which he/she can use to interpret the current actions of his opponent from similar experienced situations. In other words he/she generally knows what is coming because he/she has seen particular actions and movements hundreds and hundreds of times before. When a top player is caught out then this is generally because of a temporary lapse in concentration. He/she might have been thinking about the score or how to adjust his/her tactical approach but he/she would certainly not be concentrating sufficiently to try to identify what stroke his/her opponent was about to execute.

A rare but glaring case of lack of concentration by world class players occurred in a 1952 men's doubles match at Wimbledon when the top ranking Americans, Gardnar Mulloy and Dick Savitt, played the young 17-year-old Australians Lew Hoad and Ken Rosewall. With both Americans at the net Rosewall had been sent scurrying back several feet behind the baseline to retrieve the ball. It was quite amazing that he was able to reach the ball at all. Having done so, however, he did not play a retrieving lob but a whipped back-hand return down the centre of the court bisecting the motionless Americans. Everyone, and not least the seasoned American campaigners, were astonished. Of course, if the Americans had been concentrating then they could have dealt with the shot with ease for the stroke had been played from so far behind the baseline. The most likely explanation is that the Americans were beaten by this particular shot because it was probably something rare even in their experience. It had, therefore, not been expected. Anticipating shots which the crowds find almost unbelievable occur because the players are repeatedly doing such things in practice and are so accustomed to dealing with seemingly impossible shots that their reactions are virtually automatic. The players themselves, therefore, are seldom surprised by what happens because to them it is happening all the time.

Anticipation then, involves attending to the relevant visual cues, signs or actions of your opponent. Players can be trained or train themselves to identify these cues or signs in the visual display which is before them. This is a process which is technically known as selective attention. It has been argued that selective attention is a necessary factor in performance in sport because the brain can only handle so much information at any one time. People are quite incapable of attending to all the things that are going on around them and can only attend to a limited number. In fact it is doubtful whether human beings can really concentrate exclusively on more than one thing at once and when they try to concentrate on several things mistakes occur and their performance generally deteriorates.

As with learning to drive a car, anyone starting to learn to play tennis finds that one of the big obstacles to progress is that so many things are happening all at once and are demanding his/her attention to the extent that he/she can become confused. He/she is, for example, consciously attending to the shot he/she is making and also to the result. That is to say that he/she may be attending to how he/she is holding the racquet, how he/she means to swing it, how he/she is standing, what the coach is saying and so on. Having hit the ball he/she will be attending to its direction and distance. Soon, to improve, he/she will also have to start to attend to what his/her opponent is doing and to the speed, flight and the direction of the return. This will also mean that he/she must start to think of his/her own position on the court and what he/she should be doing to deal with his/her opponent's shot. All this means that for the beginner there is simply too much going on for him/her to be able to act efficiently and effectively. The stage at which he/she can cope will only be reached when he/she is able to select correct information from the actions of his/her opponent, that is, when he/she has reached the stage when he/she has a pretty good idea from his/her opponent's initial preparations what stroke is being attempted.

To improve further a player must also reach the position when he/she knows how successful his/her own strokes are going to be through recognizing certain relevant cues or signs and ignoring others. The highly skilled player has reached the stage when he/she does not have to watch and wait to know whether his/her own shots will be in or out. He knows immediately from the 'feel' of his/her shot pretty well what the outcome will be and sometimes will not even bother to look if he/she knows the stroke is a bad one.

It is difficult for the beginner to reach this stage because in tennis skills are continuous in nature so that two streams of information are overlapping each other. This means that the beginner is having to attend to information from two sources which is being received at the same time. And as it has been suggested earlier, people find it extremely difficult, if not impossible, to attend consciously to different sources of information presented at the same time.

Thus, in tennis the inexperienced player is severely handicapped because he/she is trying to attend to too much information. Mistakes occur, partly because of the beginner's perceptual incapacity which causes him/her to start his/her preparation after the ball has been struck, and partly because his/her brain literally is trying to deal with a bombardment of information with which it is unable to cope and so becomes confused.

On the other hand the highly skilled tennis player is able to predict a particular shot from his/her opponent as soon as he/she begins his/her preparations and certainly before the ball has been struck. Frequently he/she has only to sample information from initial actions to know the intention. In other words a few relevant cues or actions are sufficient literally to give 'the game away'. Being able to concentrate on a particular item considered essential to performance leads to a player being able to make predictions not only about the direction and flight of the ball but also its speed and swing in the air or spin off the ground.

In time the effect of effective prediction is to reduce the demands being made on his/her capacity to think and leaves him/her free to attend to essentials. It is in this way that the whole process of responding to situations is speeded up. There is less to think about and in fact to do mentally, thus a top class player is able to decide on a plan of action in a much shorter time than an average player. As a Cambridge psychologist Professor Bartlett pointed out, as long ago as 1947, a highly skilled performer has in fact more time because 'he has in a very real sense less to do than the unskilled man'.

A further factor which can influence the speed of a player's reactions concerns any uncertainty he/she feels about his opponent's shot. The obvious sources of uncertainty in a game include such factors as the speed, the flight, the direction and the spin of the ball. Doubts can also arise over the future positioning of the opponent in the court — what his/her particular tactics will be in a rally — whether for example he/she is going to move in to the net or remain on the baseline. Additionally a player may be uncertain about his/her own position in the court and whether it is the best one to deal with his/her opponent's shots. The greater the number of possibilities, the greater will be the uncertainty and the slower he/she will be to react. The player's responses will be greatly delayed or if they are quick the chances are they will be incorrect for he/she will be guessing with the odds against him/her.

Many aspects of ball games, such as the flight of the ball, the tactics of the opponent, tend to be highly structured, that is they are stereotyped, regular and consistent. Thus once a player has learned the structure or the pattern of the game any uncertainty is considerably reduced through a knowledge of what is most likely to occur. This can be achieved only by practice and is a further value of practice that is not generally appreciated. In other words, players practice not only to develop strokes and strategies but to reduce the amount of mental activity — to become more efficient in a mental sense — and thereby to speed up their reactions so as to adjust to the increased tempo of the game as it is played at the higher levels.

Practice and experience must be relevant. The ability to anticipate, to make accurate predictions stems from experience of playing at a high level. The author's own research into tennis supports the popularly held view that an important factor in improving performance is practice with players of a high standard of ability. High success in tournaments favoured players who had practised less often *but* with good players than others who had practised a great deal more but with moderate players. Indeed the study gives backing to the idea that as the promising player begins to develop practice with moderate players is of limited value when set beside the gains to be had from playing with top class players. Only by doing this is it possible to have the kind of experience that will give the player important information in terms of speed spin and tactics.

A good player will attempt to increase the uncertainty of his/her opponents and therefore their reactions by concealing his intentions. He/she is able, for example, to create uncertainty by beginning the execution of different shots with the same action. One good example is the lob and the backhand pass which may be started off with more or less identical actions. A classical example of this play in another game is the 'googly' in cricket. This is a ball which is bowled with a 'leg break' action but is in fact an 'off break' and spins off the pitch in the opposite direction to that which is perceived from the wrist action of the opponent. Top class players in any sport are not easily deceived and it follows that deceptions must be carefully concealed. International players will emphatically deal with any obvious attempt at deception and will take the advantage. Thus, dropshots in tennis have to be very cleverly disguised for if they are not the consequences are generally disastrous at the top level of play.

How Anticipation Can Be Improved

Anticipation is a skill. Skills are learned and improve with relevant practise. For anticipation to be improved therefore it is essential to practise anticipating. Ways in which to do this are now detailed below:

1   Moves that depend upon anticipation must be practised over and over again; the aim being to reach the stage that concert pianists aim for which is that a player becomes virtually incapable of making a mistake because every move is built into his/her body. Of course this is to aim for perfection which it is claimed cannot be reached. However, all good techniques get very close to it, so it has to be a long-term aim.

2   Practice must be relevant practice. In other words it rehearses actions that improve anticipation and builds effective habits that contribute to the ability to anticipate.

3   Players should aim to play with people who are a little better than themselves. Tournaments should be seen as very useful for this purpose.

4   Time should be spent studying players in action — especially those who are world class. When players are under pressure strokes are sometimes telegraphed in an obvious manner. It is therefore useful to start to look for the physical signs of a player's intentions. These can often be identified from the position of the feet and racquet head in tennis and the peculiar habits of individual players. As focusing attention on the movements of players improves anticipation there will be more time in which to execute shots. Whilst waiting for a match at tournaments, time can be well spent in studying particular players in the manner described and in trying to predict where a particular shot will go. Concentration should be directed to a player's movements and the resulting shots and not on the game itself.

5   The use of mental practice or imagery has been shown to be an effective means of improving the speed of anticipation if practised sufficiently. In this the player actually pictures himself playing and focusing his/her attention on his/her opponent's intentions. He/she is not a spectator in the exercise but is mentally imagining him/herself playing the game to the extent that there can sometimes be visible movement of the muscles involved.

Regular practice of the sort suggested begins to give results. Playing a lot of tennis against a particular person will mean that that person's game will be known well. Anticipation will generally be far better in this case than against players whose games are not known. Reactions are far quicker because it is generally possible to judge correctly what the opponent is going to do. In time the game of a particular player will come to be known backwards and the opposition will be 'caught napping' only by 'mishits' and the occasional freak shot that appears to come 'out of the blue'.

At world class level some of the best tennis ever seen and some of the highest standards ever reached were by the small band of leading professionals who trounced the rest of the world in the 1950s. This group of players, which included Gonzales, Hoad, Rosewall and Sedgeman, had played against each other day after day, year in year out. Their anticipation in play against each other improved to such a degree that remarkable rallies were the rule and not the exception for they knew each other's game inside out.

Tennis became professional in 1968 and the giants of the game had to study and learn the stroke production and repertoires of entirely new players whose techniques and skills were unfamiliar. Thus, to the amazement of everyone, Pancho Gonzales lost to the amateur Mark Cox at Bournemouth in 1968. But here was a new situation for Gonzales. The problem, a new opponent and a slow hard court very different from the faster surfaces to which he had become so accustomed for the best part of a couple of decades.

Chapter 6

Psychological Preparation of Competitors

Introduction

This chapter examines the importance of psychological preparation for competitive sport. It is argued that just as the physiological and technical preparation of the competitor takes place over a long period of time so should the psychological preparation of the competitor take place over a similar lengthy period. The overriding concerns of psychological preparation are that the competitor will learn how to handle psychological problems and will be able to perform to the best of his/her ability on the day. Emphasis is placed on seeing each match, each tournament as being just one in a long-term programme of preparation which builds up to a particular stage such as the qualifying event of an international tournament. Psychological preparation is seen as incorporating a sustained systematic approach to an attainable standard of performance.

As is repeatedly emphasized in this book results of particular matches and events of themselves should not be regarded as being of critical importance. What matters most is *how* matches or events were won or lost and therefore how can the competitor profit from the experience. Effective psychological preparation is very largely dependent on the quality of the analysis which is undertaken by the coach both in practice sessions and following competitive matches. The overriding consideration is to build on successive experiences with a view to the development of ability and the confidence to deal with the many stresses of competition in sport.

The Need for Psychological Preparation

The problem for many young sportspeople is that they simply do not have any kind of system preparation. As a result they can have little idea concerning the effectiveness of particular training methods and practice procedures. From the outset it is important for young people aiming to engage in competitive sport at national level to have close guidance and instruction from a knowledgeable coach or teacher. For as Beard and Sinclair (1980) have shown in the academic field, it is the student's early experiences at university which largely determine whether he withdraws, fails or succeeds. In sports it is often the vagueness concerning both the short-term and the long-term goals which causes people to lose interest. This view is supported by research, again in the academic field by Wankowski (1973) who found that poorly defined goals were a major factor in examination failure. One of the problems which arises in the absence of clearly defined goals is that the learner has little idea of what is expected of him. There is the feeling that he is operating in some kind of vacuum with little idea about progress or direction. This kind of situation soon becomes clouded by boredom, uncertainty and, in the case of the ambitious learner, frustration and worry.

Gaa (1971) has demonstrated the importance of having clearly defined goals. He found that people who attended weekly meetings at which goals for the week were set not only obtained higher test scores than a control group but also developed more positive attitudes towards their course programme. Arising from his research Gaa considers that the setting of clearly defined weekly goals can help to facilitate intrinsic motivation. Very few young sportspeople it seems spend much effort on any kind of systematic planning. This means that without concrete goals, especially in the short-term, it becomes difficult to assess progress towards competency in a particular sport. This almost certainly means that the individual can have but imprecise perceptions of the amount and type of practice required to meet the standards and demands of competition.

The attainment of goals provides the learner with a sense of achievement and in this way positive attitudes are developed and confidence generated. The setting of goals means that the learner now has a clear idea of what he is being required to do.

This chapter outlines a highly structured directed approach towards training and practice. Such an approach towards the competitive situation with clearly defined goals and regular feedback enhances motivation and the whole learning environment created thereby provides the sportsperson with a sense of security since in this situation uncertainty is minimal.

The Concept of Psychological Preparation

In just the same way as the physiological and technical preparation of the player takes place over a long period of time it is reasonable to argue that the psychological preparation should take place over a similar lengthy period. Performance in any sport depends on a combination of physiological, psychological, technical and tactical factors. This chapter is concerned with considerations for the coach in terms of the psychological preparation of players. Vanek (1975) proposes a system of analysis whereby the preparation of the player takes place during three broad phases, namely, pre-competition, competition and post-competition. Figure 5 illustrates this psychological continuum.

FIGURE 5
Continuum of psychological preparation

(1) LONG-TERM PRE-PREPARATION PERIOD	(2) SHORT-TERM PRE-PREPARATION PERIOD	(3) PRE-GAME PREPARATION	(4) START OF THE MATCH	(5) PERIOD OF COMPETITION	(6) POST COMPETITIVE PERIOD
PRE-COMPETITION PERIOD		COMPETITION PERIOD			POST-COMPETITION PERIOD

A consideration of Figure 5 is important because it is possible that different psychological conditions might exist within the player, and between the player and coach, at the various stages. The onset of the continuum, that is, at the beginning of phase (1) might be days, weeks, or preferably, months in advance of the start of the competitive season. There are numerous factors for the coach to consider during each of the phases and these are discussed later in the chapter. The end of phase (1) is characterized by the end of training, which might be one day, or one night before the start of competition. This is a period of introspective reflection. It is vital that during the short-term pre-start period (phase 2) the coach is available to enhance feelings of security and self-belief which should already have been carefully developed during the long-term build up. During phase (2) there should be relaxed discussion avoiding, if possible, the subject of the competition. This is possible, providing the long-term psychological preparation has been carefully developed. The onset of phase (3) is actually in the competition environment itself, and this can include contact with others in the team, the opponents as well as the technical and physiological 'warm-ups'. The major psychological consideration at this stage is to ensure that the optimum activation of the player is reached by the start of the match.

This is best achieved by having a well rehearsed 'warm-up' routine so that the player is physically relaxed yet mentally aroused to each peak performance. This type of feeling is crucial to success in important competitive events. The duration of phase (5) depends on the type of competition and can last for an hour or two, or a few days depending on the event. Tension levels will vary during this phase, depending on many factors and most of these will need regulating by the competitor without much contact with the coach until after the event. This self-regulation during the actual event is another important feature to be carefully developed in the competitor by using different build up matches or tournaments to gain experience of self-control prior to playing in those matches which are seen by the competitor and the coach as the major goals for the particular season. This is an important area of preparation and will be discussed later in the chapter. In the post-competitive period, phase (6), it is recommended *not* to analyze the competition. Detailed consideration of a match is best left to the next training session when arousal levels will be lower. In this way any assessment is likely to be more clinically accurate than an immediate post-match appraisal.

The overall effect of these procedures is to regulate the psychic state of the individual. The methods of achieving this vary, but can be grouped approximately as:

(1) Biological   —   for example, appropriate food, sleep.

(2) Pharmacological —   for example, administering relaxants, stimulants.

(3) Physiological   —   for example, relaxation exercises.

(4) Psychological   —   for example, desensitization of the individual in specific situations. (The object here is the development of secure self-confidence.)

The whole basis behind having a knowledge of each of the above factors is the view that the optimum psychic state enables the individual player to produce his/her best performance on the required occasion. Some of the factors are closely linked and the coach will need to be aware of each of them if he/she is to function effectively in the area of psychological preparation.

Clearly the role of the coach is crucial during the preparation of a player for competitive play and this can best be illustrated by saying that the relationship between psychological preparation and motivation during a major game is similar to the relationship between the amount of training and technical practice and the actual output in a match. Since the physiological output during a match is effected by motivation then the factors which contribute towards the player's motivation are crucially important. The manipulation of these factors could be described as the psychological handling of the player during the match.

Even a lengthy theoretical consideration of the influences which affect the psychic state of the player, or group of players, fails to explain how these ideas can be communicated to the individuals concerned. Throughout the preparation and competition periods direct links between organization, training and motivation can be traced. Clearly the coach is the medium for this communication and his/her personality will govern the process. Just as players react individually in different situations so will the coach. Thus, interactions between situations and players will be different for each coach. That is not to say, however, that two coaches strategically speaking will not be suggesting similar tactics in a similar game situation. The essential, and important difference between coaches is the way he/she explains tactics to the player. The timing of the procedure, in order to optimize activation is usually the key to successful psychological handling.

The coach needs to know how to influence the players in his/her charge. This may be achieved directly, by such activities as explanation of the rationale behind a particularly arduous training session, or by discussion with players, or by domination. These are largely conscious actions which may or may not be successful with individuals, but, equally important, may be aspects of unconscious communication. Subliminal communication is an exchange of interpersonal behaviour which has been examined in some depth by Argyle (1967) in relation to social motivation and for many club players, may be the reason for participation in the game.

Returning to the original continuum of psychological preparation, it is useful to examine ways in which the coach can utilize techniques in a practical way. Considering each period in turn:

Let us examine:

(1)   Long-term pre-preparation period —
coach uses social and communication skills to motivate each player in each training circumstance.

(2)   Short-term pre-game period —
coach manipulates atmosphere in order to induce relaxation with a view to controlling the psychic state of the player.

117

(3) Period of start conditions —
coach and players seek to control level of arousal in order to reach optimal level.

(4) Period of competition —
players seek to control their own levels of activation using relaxation and attention control techniques acquired in training. In some circumstances the coach has an opportunity to influence the psychic state of a player during a match providing he/she has access. The opportunity occurs, for example, in the Davis and Wightman Cup competitions when the players change ends.

(5) Post-competitive period —
analysis of successes/failures in the competition. Period of resolution and direction of attention to key points in the game where psychic state influences performance.

It must be remembered that even the most sophisticated psychological techniques in training will be of limited value unless the player sees them as directed towards producing the best possible performance on the occasion of an important match. Matches must be seen in some hierarchical order by the player if he is attempting to break through in two or three major tournaments during a season. It is impossible to reach either a physiological or psychological peak for every game and the coach must seek with the player to see results in the perspective of a long-term plan. This is essential if effective long-term psychological preparation is to have a beneficial effect on a player's performance in key matches.

The Pre-Competition Period

The main feature of any long-term preparation is to develop the player's ability to cope with unexpected circumstances in order to maintain progress towards the ultimate goal to be reached by the end of the tournament season. The ability to learn to cope with all possible distractors is probably never realized by any player. But, through a constant learning process, players develop a knowledge and an experience of the behaviour required to handle the various stresses which do occur in tournament play. The major point to emphasize is that each match, each tournament should be seen as being just one in a long-term programme of preparation which builds up to a particular stage such as the qualifying event of a major international tournament or at junior level it might be the Grass Courts Championships at Eastbourne or the Orange Bowl event in the USA. The tournament programme must be seen as incorporating a systematic approach to an attainable standard of performance. The lesson is to be drawn from other sports, such as athletics and boxing. Sebastian Coe and Steve Ovett, for example, use a series of athletic events throughout the season as preparation for the Olympic Games, the Commonwealth Games or the European Championships. Each event in which these athletes compete is seen as an integral part of their preparation for the major competition. Thus competitors must see each tournament as providing an opportunity to learn and profit from the experience. Each match should be seen as an opportunity to develop ability. The idea is to analyze the match and then to simulate in practice those critical conditions which operated in the match. For example, if a player went into a match he was expecting to win only to find himself suddenly love-4 down, then practice matches should be played with the score at love-4. What did the player do in the actual match? Did he/she approach the situation in a positive way — that is by trying to work out how he/she could win, or did his/her concentration fail? Concentration falls when players begin to cast blame for their performance on the court, the racquets, the weather or they start to think of the social consequences of defeat in terms of what people will say and think and how their standing in the game will be affected. If there is a deterioration in concentration then practice sessions should simulate the match condition with the player being instructed to keep his attention externally focused — that is he/she is seeking ways in which he/she can win, which is the positive approach. By simulating this same situation in practice you learn how to cope, how to behave and how to act and in this way you develop the emotional maturity, the confidence to deal effectively with such situations in future matches. As is repeatedly emphasized in this book for the aspiring international player, results of matches of themselves should not be regarded as being of critical importance. What matters most is *how* matches were won or lost and therefore how can the player profit from the experience. Here it is the quality of the analysis which is important. The analysis could centre on attitudes, concentration, strategy, technique and confidence. The overriding consideration is to build on successive experiences with a view to the development of ability and the emotional maturity to deal effectively and positively with the various stresses of tournament competition.

In order to develop the ability to cope with the competition the coach follows a two-stage process. Firstly the pre-competition and competition situations are analyzed in detail. Long-term pre-competition factors include training facilities, time available, availability of practice partners and so on, whilst shorter term factors include actual pre-event details such as travelling arrangements, accommodation, audience characteristics and the personal habits of the player. Basically the coach has to analyze both stages of pre-competition and determine what will happen and what could happen and then develop a coping behaviour strategy. These strategies should be developed in a language the player understands and must emphasize the behaviour to be done in a positive task-orientated way. Each tournament will need to be planned in detail and cannot be treated in a haphazard way if long-term preparation is to be beneficial in terms of maximum performance 'on the day'.

The usual procedure for developing the ability to cope is actually to practise it following a planned, stepwise introduction of competitive behaviour and occasional distractions during the build up to the main goals selected for the season. Thus, once the player has developed the capacity to cope successfully in one situation another more complex situation can be introduced. This phasing and planning of selected tournaments and matches must be a very carefully thought-out strategy by the coach. This development of the coping ability should probably occupy as much time as the training programme or physical development or skill training.

The player's ability to cope is determined by past experience and the coach has three types of practices available:

1   Actual Competition:
Competing in a variety of situations yields first-hand practice of coping for the player. However, the outcomes of these can have a positive or negative effect on the player's capacity to cope. One way of assuring a positive effect is to watch the player closely during the event. Following the match or tournament in the post-competitive period the coach and the player then analyze what can be learned from the experience.

2   Contrived Situations:
Usually, this takes the form of a simulated event with a full practice of variables such as change in rest times, larger matches than usual, no spectators, playing on a court with a poor surface and so on. The essential thing if the contrived situation is to have a positive effect on the coping capacity is that the experiences should be seen by the player to be of benefit. If not, they need to be repeated until the player can handle a range of distractions comfortably.

3   Mental Rehearsal:

This entails using mental imagery of the various situations and events. It is important that the coach has a knowledge of the frequency of the sessions which the player may be using at their own discretion. Research into superior athletes has demonstrated that they have used this technique as much as possible prior to the onset of competition. Research also seems to indicate that the mental rehearsal of coping behaviours is most effective if it is undertaken whilst the player is totally relaxed.

Basically, two types of behaviour need to be developed for successful psychological preparation, those which are required before the match and those actually required during the match. The development of coping strategies in training must include both types and in the long term should lessen the threat of the contest. In a tournament which might last over several days it is best to segmentalize the contest into logical parts each with its own goals and coping reactions.

Short-term Preparation Period and Pre-game Preparation

The techniques involved during the short-term period and the period immediately before the game include an analysis of all the activities undertaken by the player during this time period. In the case of tournaments where the player might be away from home it might last for a few days. Under other more usual circumstances, it might only last a few hours. This pre-event period involves the coach in two types of strategy each of which make a significant contribution to the psychic state of the individual. These are activities which could be classified under general planning and those which are specific to the particular event.

Under the concept of general planning the sort of distractions which the player has to be helped to tolerate might include the pre-match meal, timing of the meal, the type of physical activities to undertake prior to moving to the location of the game, details of equipment and travel, mental rehearsal programme and, very importantly from the coach's point of view, when to check with the player for anxiety levels. A particular characteristic of this type of planning, especially noticeable in top players is that they have this familiar thoroughly practised routine. There are a range of techniques available to the coach to help establish this routine which should be a feature of every competition the player enters. These include some of the relaxation procedures discussed in another section of the book. Interaction with other players, or small groups of people all help to reduce stress levels because the presence of others often eases tension. It is quite feasible that the coach might have to control some members of the group in some way to avoid possible conflicts. If any loss of confidence occurs it can have disastrous results on the forthcoming performance so the coach might need to use relaxation techniques along with positive self-imagery to counteract any loss. Another particularly useful technique to enhance self-image is to run through some practice drills that the player enjoys and performs well. Following this there can be an evaluation period to reinforce a positive self image.

Activities specific to the event surround the actual location of the match once the player has arrived. Once again the routine concept is used by adjusting to such things as the suitability of the court, the expected strengths and weaknesses of the opponent and match strategy. The latter two will have been discussed well before but warm–up and arousal procedures may have to include reference to these if the coach suspects the player is not sufficiently aroused or to use the American jargon 'psyched up' to perform at his/her peak.

Many top players begin their on-site preparation with relaxation practices which produce a level of arousal, which is controlled and totally familiar to the player. This is followed by a 'warm-up' where the temperature of the muscles is increased to a suitable working efficiency and the suppleness of the working joints is slowly increased to their maximum range. It is very useful if a player can follow the physiological/psychological warm-up routine on an outside court, not against the actual opponent as part of the typical knock-up. It is important that the players keep active and warm right up to the moment of going on court. Mental rehearsals should be practised in order to maintain concentration and as the start of the game approaches the coach should seek to keep the players away from well-meaning visitors. A characteristic of top players is that they are so familiar with this build-up that they are able to do so entirely on their own and reach a state of match readiness at the right moment on several big occasions during the season. Much experience is needed to achieve this capability. It is often shown by young, very talented, players that they cannot match the consistent high standards of more experienced players although on the day they may be unbeatable. This is because they have not developed the consistent coping strategy in terms of concentration and a positive approach which is needed for long-term success.

Competition Period

This is the behaviour during the actual competition from the moment the player comes under the control of the officials to the end of the match. This phase of the psychological continuum would also include warm-down and recovery periods but detailed analysis is best left to the post competition period if it is to be used effectively in a less emotional atmosphere in order to improve future behaviours.

Research evidence seems to suggest that achieving a short-term goal in a tournament, which is seen as part of a plan towards a longer term goal, stimulates the player to further effort. Motivation is maintained with respect to the necessary behaviour required to achieve the goal. Many successful coaches argue that achieving a goal in the competition environment tends to improve the self-image of the player and raises expectations of success. Once this positive feeling has been engendered it is possible to build it up step-wise towards the long-term goal of the season. Many experienced coaches find that a high level of arousal sustained for too long, or more importantly called for too often can leave the player feeling flat just at the vital moment in the season when the big game approaches. Thus, it is critically important that the coach identifies with the player the level of arousal needed for the particular game and that it is seen as just a part of the build-up towards the long-term goal. For example, in other words, each tournament, each match should be seen in its proper perspective as part of a programme of preparation for the major events to come.

One way to tackle a match is to divide it up into several discreet units each with its own goal. The units might be groups of three, five, seven games or whatever. The theory is that the player enters the match with the sole aim of achieving the goal set for the first unit, which might be, for example, winning the first three games. If this occurs then the next stage can be pursued with increasing confidence. If the first goal is not achieved then the strategy, the approach, must be adjusted to enable the player to get back on target for the ultimate goal which he/she has been set.

This sort of approach is recommended in cases where somebody is playing a vastly superior player. Having a goal, say a particular number of games to win, gives the competitor a yardstick by which to measure and evaluate progress.

Most psychological strategy during competition deals with the concentration upon the technical aspects of the game, the skills and the nature of attacking and defending play. Research evidence indicates that concentration on these aspects of the game should occupy about two-thirds of all the thought content during the time the player is on court. The areas on which thoughts should be focused during the match should include such things as analysis of the opponent's play, an effective court strategy which in a prolonged testing match may have to be adjusted from time to time. Strategies really need to be planned beforehand. For these to be effective a close knowledge of the opponent's strengths and weaknesses is a necessary prerequisite. An excellent example of intelligent psychological strategy was seen in the Wimbledon men's final of 1975 when Arthur Ashe beat the favourite and title-holder Jimmy Connors. Here was a classic example of a player using his own strengths to exploit the opponent's weaknesses to the full.

In the majority of cases young tournament players, even senior ones, go on court with little in the way of any pre-conceived plan on how best to win the match. Each match is invariably approached in the same way and a thorough analysis of the opponent's strengths and weaknesses very rarely occurs.

Loss of concentration can be a feature of any prolonged and testing match. With increasing mental and physical fatigue concentration tends to deteriorate with the player starting to make casual returns and becoming increasingly slower to react. He/she ceases to be sufficiently involved mentally in the match and a run of several games, a set even can be lost very quickly indeed. Concentration can be adversely affected from the physical discomfort arising from tensed and tired muscles. With fatigue attention becomes increasingly distracted by all kinds of irrelevant stimuli such as the crowd, the court and the idiosyncracies of the opponent. Fatigue effects become greater as the mental demands on the individual increase. Thus the highly skilled player will be less vulnerable to fatigue effects than the less skilled player because the task of winning is less difficult. Further, as we saw in chapter 5, the anticipation of the highly skilled player is so superior to that of the unskilled that he/she has less to do mentally and therefore he/she expends less energy. This is because he has become so efficient in predicting what will happen and can 'read' the opponent's game almost effortlessly. It sometimes happens that when two players of differing abilities meet the scores can be level pegging for perhaps a set or so only for the inferior player to fall sharply away as the match continues so that it becomes virtually a rout in the end. This situation may well arise from mental fatigue arising from the constant pressure of trying to recognize in sufficient time the intentions of the superior player. Without sufficient experience this is very difficult indeed. In trying to speed up reactions mistakes are made through an inability to anticipate correctly. The inferior player starts to guess, there is a lack of coordination, despair almost in this for him/her, an unfamiliar situation.

The onset of fatigue may also be accompanied by feelings of anxiety and insecurity with a player beginning to worry about his/her performance. This, in turn, leads to a further deterioration in performance since concentration is again adversely affected. With fatigue it becomes more difficult to sustain concentration and judgment is impaired. Fatigue effects tend to be greater for new situations than for familiar situations. Stress, for example, is likely to be greater when playing against a particular player for the first time or when playing on a new surface or for somebody making his/her debut on the centre court at Wimbledon.

An important function of practice, therefore, is to equip a player not only physically but mentally and emotionally for long, exacting tournament matches. The idea is gradually to build up the physical and mental demands of practice sessions so that the player learns to accommodate to the extreme pressures of competitive play. Thus practice matches in the end should be as exacting, if not more so, than competitive matches. Physical demands can be met through various forms of pressure training. Mental and emotional capacities can be developed by operating a system of handicaps, rewards and penalties. These can readily be devised by the ingenious coach. Players can practise serving at 0-30 down for example. Two points can be awarded for serving aces and none for short services. Indeed, there are a whole variety of strategies available which can be devised to suit the psychological needs of individual players so that they become increasingly psychologically 'tough' or resilient and, at the same time, cultivate a positive, thrusting approach to the competitive match situation.

The coach can develop a player's capacity to handle such problems as a loss of concentration by pointing out where this loss is operating. It is a question of keeping the attention externally focused throughout the match. Positive mental imagery can also be employed to sustain concentration. Thus the player can visualize before he/she serves where he/she intends the ball to go into the service court for example. Positive mental imagery prevents the mind from wandering since it limits the amount of interference from other variables such as worrying about performance. Mental imagery becomes relatively easy with practice and it can be employed throughout a match, particularly when changing ends. Furthermore, imagery of playing a good shot not only helps to sustain concentration but it also reinforces feelings of confidence. If a player is suffering from mental fatigue and is under-aroused then the use of positive self-statements can help raise arousal levels. Conversely, some players may have become fatigued by being over-aroused and have been too tense from the start of the match. Thus an individual approach to the physical and psychological needs of players is essential. Players simply cannot all be helped in the same way. A detailed post-match analysis, therefore, is imperative for the player to develop the capacity to learn to handle the loss of concentration.

Role of the Coach in the Psychological Preparation of the Young Player

Botterill (1978) argues that there are two areas in which psychology contributes towards the long-term preparation of players for competition:

(a)   maximizing the players' performance;

(b)   maximizing the players' personal growth and development.

Recent research has indicated that there is an extremely important relationship between the two areas. In order to make significant progress towards maximizing playing performances, attention must be paid to the young player's personal growth and development. The psychological stresses of the modern world of tennis are tremendous and the majority of players who perform consistently well are those who are psychologically healthy and mature. On analysis, they seem to be able to keep cool, adapt to rapidly changing game situations and yet maintain self-discipline and a committed attitude towards the game. Examples of men players with these characteristics which spring readily to mind from past years are Stan Smith, Rod Laver, Ken Rosewall, Björn Borg, Roscoe Tanner, John Newcombe, Arthur Ashe, Tony Roche, Manuel Orantes and the doubles pair Paul McNamee and Peter McNamara. More recently Mats Wilander, Stefan Edberg and Miroslav Mecir typify this approach to the game, also Anders Jarryd. Among the women there is, of course, the implacable Chris Evert, Martina Navratilova, Steffi Graf and, during the sixties, Evonne Cawley (Goolagong).

The coach's role is to help youngsters to develop these characteristics because without help it is unlikely that they will all occur automatically. In the long run, it is the young player who will have to cope on his/her own under pressure, and in order for him/her to be able to do this effectively the coach must pay attention to the personal growth of the players in his/her care. Research into behaviour modification seems to indicate that by actively involving the player from the start in planning a behaviour change, by discussing why certain behaviour changes are important coaches can produce more consistent effective behaviour improvement than by simply trying to maximize performance before a game, which frequently results in inconsistent patterns of play. In any psychological situation where there are so many variables, such as the attitude of the spectators, the opponent, the officials and varying weather conditions. The only sensible thing for the coach to do is to develop the player's own ability to control the situation and to regulate his/her own arousal levels and focus of attention.

From a psychological perspective the concept of planning a seasonal programme or even a more extended programme has important implications for both coach and player. Despite the fact that this is probably the most important facet of coaching it is often the one which is most neglected. There is often little communication between coach and player. Frequently the season begins with the player having little understanding of what it is all about. He/she knows little of the coach's goals and expectations nor does he/she have any clear idea of his/her own goals and expectations. It is useful to think about the forthcoming season in three ways:

1 Areas of concern for the player.

2 What specific goals can be set in each of these areas.

3 How will these goals be achieved — what strategies will be employed.

If the coach's goals are incompatible with those of the player then pre-season is the time to discuss this and to find an acceptable solution. Ideally coach and player should work in harmony and plan a programme for the season which is mutually acceptable.

Having established a comprehensive list of areas of concern together with some specific goals and strategies, the second in the preparation is to have some planning sessions with the player where discussion should focus upon such issues as

1 What the season is all about.

2 Major worries of the player about the forthcoming season.

3 The goals which can be established to help solve the areas of concern.

4 The strategy which is to be employed in order to achieve these goals.

An example of a possible approach to this type of psychological planning is shown in Figure 6.

FIGURE 6

Area of concern	Specific goal	Strategy
1 Match fitness	1 Be able to perform a series of short sprints in a certain time.	1 Not entered for competition until the target has been achieved.
	2 Be able to go round a circuit of exercises in a set time.	
2 Lack of skill	1 Be able to top-spin lob consistently under pressure.	1 Regular drills and practices.
	2 Be able to move in to volley hard after service.	2 Participate in practice sessions with better players.
3 Behaviour with officials	1 No arguing with match officials.	1 Loss of playing time by violators.
		2 Not entered for future competition.

Obviously, there are numerous areas of the game situation which might concern the player and whilst the analysis of these might be a little false before the season begins, it does at least provide a framework and creates the right motivational climate for discussion to take place as the season unfolds. It is very important, even at this stage of psychological preparation, to state goals in specific, measurable, behavioural terms. The coach must push the player in setting meaningful, realistic achievable goals and this aspect of coaching requires considerable insight into both the nature of the game and the nature of the player.

The final stage in the long-term psychological preparation is actually making the plans work. Here the coach's role is to encourage behaviour which is consistent with the goals which have been established. It is crucial that the coach's behaviour is consistent with the stated goals and strategies; this is especially important in coaching young players who are looking for leadership behaviour models from the coach. During this final stage a periodic review of the stated goals and strategies enables the coach to provide feedback to the player. The review can be a source of pride or reinforcement or an opportunity to focus attention on the reasons for failure and a possible adjustment of goals.

The techniques outlined have several advantages over a more haphazard system of long-term preparation namely:

1 Clarified goals help coach and player to see what the season is all about and exactly what is *expected* of them.

2 Long-term motivation will be enhanced.

3 The player's self-confidence will be improved.

4 Problem behaviours will be reduced or eliminated.

5 There will be increased 'rapport' between coach and player.

Chapter 7

Psychological Factors and Performance in Competitive Sport

Introduction

This chapter reviews some of the psychological factors which research shows are related to performance in competitive sport generally. It seems to be the general view among players of ball games that the hallmark of the champion is the capability continually to play the 'big points' well. Since on average there is generally little difference in the quality of the play at any one stage of a game, this rather suggests that on the 'big points' psychological factors assume critical importance. There are, of course, so many factors which operate to determine championship performance and such marked differences between players that it is simply not possible to generalize. Certain trends and relationships have, however, been identified which have important implications for the training and development of champions in sport.

The main section of this chapter is concerned with the importance of psychological factors for achievement and performance in competitive sport. In particular the discussion ranges over such variables as personality and adjustment, tournament experience, counselling and psychological support, social pressures and persistence. Other variables such as motivation, mental preparation, confidence and concentration receive extensive attention elsewhere and are not discussed in this chapter.

Myths and Oversimplistic Viewpoints

Myths and oversimplistic viewpoints abound in the literature concerned with competitive sport. They represent a superficial analysis. They stem mainly from ignorance and are resorted to in a vain attempt to explain the performance feats or lack of them of individual competitors. The following is a sample which has come to the attention of the author in recent years: 'Confidence is everything', 'It's all in the mind', 'It's guts that counts', 'Competition's the thing', 'Toughen them up', 'Start them young'. In fact, many factors combine to determine championship performance. These include, amongst others — technical ability and skill, speed of movement, physical fitness, persistence, anticipation, concentration and the temperamental capacity to withstand the rigours of continual competitive play.

The Importance of Psychological Factors

It is evident that the greater the stress, the greater the need to succeed the more important do psychological factors become in determining performance in the competitive match situation. For those trying to make their way in tennis, for example, there is no doubt that the basic philosophy pervading the tennis tournament scene is that 'winning isn't everything — it's the only thing'. Thus in this context the psychological pressures are immense. At the qualifying events of the major championship events tennis offers one of the most extreme forms of competition in contemporary society. The qualifying event for Wimbledon is more a test of temperamental robustness than of skill. It is a great 'leveller' and most players see competing in the event as a more intimidating prospect than the championships themselves. There is manifest relief when they find that they don't have to qualify. Only wins count.[1] Wins equate with success and losses with failure. It is at this level and the major national junior championships with players striving to become recognized that the stresses are greatest. This is evidenced by the unusually high number of unforced errors in the matches and the negative behavioural and emotional reactions, which frequently accompany the behaviour of many of our players.

Paradoxically at the top of the game the pressures outside the major world championships are not nearly so great. The game here has become something of a circus or an exclusive club, with the professionals sharing in the prize money whether they win or lose. The circuit routine week by week takes place in a relatively friendly and relaxed atmosphere because the pressures simply are less than in those tournaments where players are striving for recognition and acceptance.

An exception to this is the performance at Wimbledon and elsewhere of some of the few British players of world class. Their results are indicative of the disruptive effects which extreme stress can have on standards of play. They seem so often to be at odds with themselves.

John Lloyd, for example, had for a time clearly lost confidence in his ability to win matches and his self-doubt and lack of any conviction were obvious to all who watched him play. Similarly, the immensely talented Virginia Wade lost to vastly inferior players on several occasions in the major world tournaments and came nowhere near to doing justice to her ability. Sue Barker was another player of world class who often failed to produce her best form. It is as though all these three players were going on court hoping to win rather than intending to win. Having the intention to win is the very hallmark of the confident competitor. In effect players who have lost confidence in their ability are really having to overcome not only their opponents but their own inhibiting dispositions. Players without confidence lose matches they should really win because they can't relax, they are too tense and anxious and they become over-concerned with their own game and how they are playing. Their attention tends to be internally focused when it should be exclusively externally focused. They worry about losing instead of concentrating their attention on the opponent and how to win. They think about avoiding the double-fault rather than thinking about what service will cause the opponent the most difficulty. As a result they become hesitant, indecisive, slow to react because of a lowering in attention and concentration. American Davis Cup players at one time were told before they went on court to 'Hit hard', 'Watch the ball' and 'Don't think'. It was good advice.

Tim Galwey (1974) in his book *Tennis the Inner Game* stresses this point. The idea is just to let things happen, to become thoroughly immersed in the game and lost in the action. Routines and strokes which have been practised extensively, which have been overlearned to the extent that they are virtually automatic will happen, the body will respond. Thinking consciously about a skilled movement will result in a deterioration in the performance. As with driving a car, for example, many of the movements have in a sense been forgotten which becomes apparent when we come to teach somebody to drive, for example, changing gear. Telling a player 'Not to think' refers to his/her strokes and not to tactics or strategy which he/she should be constantly thinking about as he/she assesses and reassesses his/her opponent's strengths and weaknesses. Some discussion of the advice concerning the avoidance of conscious thought during stroke production is perhaps helpful.

Skilled performance is characterized by way of explanation by fluency, smoothness of movement and economy of effort. This is the result of extensive practice. With practice, movements become easier and easier until the stage is reached when actions are carried out automatically, almost unconsciously. When a player starts to learn a new movement or action, such as a backhand smash, he/she is at first very consciously aware of his/her behaviour. As he/she continues to practise the stroke, it will gradually become more and more automatic. All sorts of daily activities, such as dressing, eating, writing, are examples of skilled actions which are carried out automatically. If conscious thought were ever given to these activities they would become less smooth and less efficient. Teaching someone to change gear in a car is perhaps a good example of this. We often find that at first a verbal explanation of the action is surprisingly not exactly spontaneous and that for a moment experienced car drivers have forgotten what they do. Thus consciously thinking about playing a stroke leads to a regression in performance and further under the stress of competition, even well consolidated strokes may begin to break down. Drawing a player's attention to a particular stroke in which he may lack confidence is a ploy which a few ruthless opponents have been known to use with this very intention in mind.

With regard to arousal, the ideal combination is, of course, to be mentally alert and yet physically relaxed 'As loose as ashes' as one American writer once put it. It is not an easy combination to obtain since body and mind states are interrelated. Thus in a physically relaxed state there is the tendency to be mentally relaxed so that a player will not be attending sufficiently and failing to 'read' his opponent's game sufficiently well for his reactions to be effective. Similarly, with the mind very alert there is the tendency for the body to become tense, for muscles to become overtaxed so that movements and strokes become less smooth with a tendency to hurry and to snatch at the ball.[2]

Mark Cox is an example of a British player who invariably did justice to his ability in the major tournaments. His concentration was good. A compact, efficient player who contrived to play consistently well against top world class opposition. His concentration was good because his attention was externally focused. He was composed and failed to become over-concerned about bad calls, net cords, bad bounces, faults with racquets but was able to forget such things and, in common language, to 'Get on with the game'.

Psychological Factors and Performance

Whilst it is possible to identify certain psychological factors which can have a considerable influence upon a person's play, it must be remembered that there is a certain intrinsic variability in the human performance of highly skilled activities. Scores from one intelligence testing to another are likely to show some slight variation for most people for example and for no readily identifiable reason the play of competitors in sport is likely to vary from one match to another. Things seem to go right on some days and we feel good. At other times nothing seems to go right on the important points. Luck, of course, is also a factor affecting performance in tennis. With these qualifications in mind the following psychological factors are likely to be important determinants of performance. Some of these, including motivation, mental preparation, confidence and concentration, have been given considerable attention in other chapters and are not discussed in this section.

1 Personality and adjustment
2 Past experience of tournament play
3 Availability of psychological support/counselling
4 Social pressures
5 Persistence
6 Confidence and concentration
7 Mental preparation
8 Motivation

Personality Factors

In recent years there have been an increasing number of research investigations, mainly in America, concerned with the relationship between achievement in sport and personality factors. The early research in this field was concerned with investigating the possibility that individual differences in performance might in some way be related to personality variables. The impression that personality could be a factor in achievement in sport derives some support from the fact that there is now evidence to show that the personalities of champion players differ from those of moderate players and also that there are often differences in the personalities of participants in sport and non-participants.

There are two major difficulties in this area of research. One of these is the problem of the difficulties of personality measurement and the other is that motor learning is task specific or, in other words, individual learning ability generally varies from task to task.

A number of self-report tests or personality questionnaires have been developed to measure various personality factors such as anxiety, sociability and aggression. Cattell's tests claim to measure 16 personality factors. These have been widely used in research investigations in sport. There are certain well known limitations to this inferential approach.

The accuracy of self-report tests for example is frequently influenced by such factors as honesty and the desire to create a favourable impression or, in other words, to be seen in a 'good light'. Even when people try to be honest, however, the answers they give may not be objectively true. Neurotic people, for example, have a tendency to exaggerate their defects. They complain about aches and pains and about sleep problems to an objectively excessive degree. Generally they tend to be more self-deprecative than people of a calmer and more stable disposition. Scores on self-report measures are also influenced by such factors as the personality of the tester, the time of day, experience of previous tests and temporary moodswings. In a review of self-report instruments to assess anxiety Tryon (1980) argues that the tests contain cues for the respondents who may be influenced by the demand characteristics of the situation. Tryon, in fact, concludes by saying the tests are easily 'fakeable'. Clearly self-report tests used in isolation are inadequate with respect to individual measurement but they do distinguish between large numbers of people to the extent that we can know that Group A, on the average, is more anxious, extraverted or aggressive than Group B, for example. Despite these certain well-known limitations of this inferential approach it is generally accepted that the self-report technique is a useful method in the assessment of personality for research purposes using large numbers of people. With single individuals they can be a useful guide and may be employed in conjunction with other methods of assessment such as interviews and systematic observation. When given on an individual basis in which 'good rapport' is established, personality questionnaires serve as a useful 'lead in' to the problems of the sports competitor and in this sense provide a valuable instrument for the sports psychologist.

It was mentioned earlier that a second main obstacle concerning identifying relationships which may exist between personality factors and achievement in sport is the fact that motor learning is task specific, which makes the reaching of any generalized conclusions difficult. It is clear from research evidence that people do not possess a general ability for the learning of sports skills. Bachman (1961), Oxendine (1967) and Marteniuk (1969) have all demonstrated that an individual's learning ability varies from task to task. Marteniuk argues the case very strongly and suggests that the ability to learn two separate motor skills will only be similar when the two skills involve very much the same actions. He points to the futility of looking for a factor of general motor ability. The position is sumed up neatly by Henry (1956 p.68–69) who states:

. . . The evidence from controlled research gives no indication that there is any quantitively important unitary function that can be called general coordination. On the contrary it must be conceded that coordinations are highly specific — it is largely a matter of chance whether an individual who is highly coordinated in one type of performance will be well or poorly coordinated in another. This does not, of course, exclude the possibility of a few 'natural athletes' who are so fortunate as to be gifted with a large number of specifics or the 'motor moron', that unfortunate individual who has few or none.

Quoted in Lawther (1968) *The Learning of Physical Skills,* New Jersey, Prentice-Hall (p.131).

Extraversion and Neuroticism

Eysenck (1947) postulates the existence of two major orthogonal personality dimensions referred to frequently as types to emphasize the broad descriptions of their meaning. These dimensions are termed extraversion – introversion and neuroticism or stability – instability. Strong support for the independence of extraversion and neuroticism comes from an investigation by Farley (1967) who found no significant correlation between these personality dimensions. The research indicates (Eysenck, 1947) that the distribution among individuals of these two dimensions is continuous and follows the normal curve.

There is evidence to show that a strong hereditary influence underlies both extraverted and neurotic behaviour. Research by Shields (1962), for example, showed substantial correlations (r=.60) on various tests of extraversion and neuroticism for identical twins reared apart. The coefficients were, if anything, higher than for identical twins reared together and certainly higher than in the case of fraternal twins. Eysenck and Eysenck (1969) consider that the predisposition to both neurotic and extraverted behaviour is largely determined by the particular constitution of the autonomic and central nervous systems. Neuroticism, they suggest, is closely bound up with the lability of the autonomic nervous system and it seems clear that the degree of lability present largely controls an individual's level of activation or arousal, which in turn it is suggested controls the extent and persistence to which an individual reacts to stimuli. Research by Davies *et al* (1963) suggests that neurotics react more strongly to stimuli and are more readily aroused than stable individuals when stress is applied, and that the level of arousal in introverts is habitually higher than in extraverts.

Much of the research has been an attempt to show that a

relationship exists between personality factors and various constitutional and fundamental aspects of behaviour. Thus there is physiological evidence to the effect that the sedation threshold is higher in introverts than in extraverts, i.e., introverts need a greater amount of narcotic drug to reach a given level of sedation (Claridge and Herrington, 1960). Howarth (1963) indicated that a further distinction between extraverts and introverts could be noted with tolerance for pain. His findings revealed that extraverts were able to keep one leg raised for significantly longer periods than introverts and this would seem to indicate a higher pain threshold for extraverts.

Other research findings show that introverts have longer after images (Holland and Gomez, 1963) and that they are superior on vigilance tasks (Hogan, 1966). With regard to both arousal theory and cortical excitation/inhibition theory we should expect introverts to form conditioned responses more easily than extraverts. This is in fact the case and the experimental evidence is considerable and generally uniform (Franks, 1957; Vogel, 1961). Finally, in accordance with prediction, both Corcoran (1964) and Eysenck and Eysenck (1967) found that introverts react more strongly to sensory stimulation. In the latter enquiry the results revealed a substantial negative correlation of -0.7 between salivary reaction and extraversion, the regression being linear over the whole range of extraversion scores.

Experimental psychologists appear to have neglected the neuroticism dimension, the main finding relevant to this study being the speed with which neurotics become aroused relative to stable individuals under conditions of stress (Davies *et al*, 1963).

The evidence cited suggests that important physiological differences exist between personality types in terms of levels of arousal or activation of the autonomic nervous system.

Evidence cited above shows that extraverts have a lower level of arousal than introverts and that neurotic individuals are more easily aroused than stable people. However, the position is not a simple one. Blake (1967), for example, showed that levels of arousal might vary within individuals according to the time of day, and Colquohoun and Corcoran (1964) found the performance of introverts relative to extraverts to be superior in the morning but that extraverts did better in the evening. Moreover an individual's level of arousal for a particular activity is likely to vary with his ability for that activity. Thus although more difficult tasks lead to higher levels of arousal (Denny, 1966) the difficulty of a particular task will vary among individuals according to their separate abilities. More able subjects, therefore, are less likely to be affected by anxiety than less able because the task will create less arousal.

An interesting research finding is that extraverts perform better than introverts in the presence of distracting stimuli (Howarth, 1969). This may help to account for the general superiority of extraverts in competitive events which are frequently performed in the presence of distracting stimuli which are present in the form of an audience and other competitors.

The fact that extraverts are less easily distracted could be attributed to their habitually lower levels of arousal. The extravert, during performance, is less sensitive to external irrelevant stimuli and will tend to be ignorant or insensitive about the reactions of other people towards him. The introvert, on the other hand, with a higher level of arousal and thus more sensitive to external stimuli might well become over-aroused or over-anxious in the presence of others. Laboratory findings concerning the effects of distraction on performance could well have implications for the teaching of sports skills.

The introduction of stress to a learning situation in the form of a more difficult task or of various incentives involves action of the autonomic nervous system with an increase in the level of arousal. Thus mild stress is likely to be associated with an improvement in performance and severe stress with a loss in performance due to individuals becoming over-aroused. Occasionally, Welford (1968) considers that severe stress could result in panic and a complete breakdown in learning and a return to a more primitive or earlier form of response.

Introverts, in whom level of arousal is habitually higher than extraverts, and neurotics, who are easily aroused, would appear to be particularly vulnerable to stressful conditions. This might help to account for the preponderance of stable extraverts who achieve international honours in sport. However, the position is an extremely complex one. Levels of anxiety or arousal not only vary between individuals for a particular stressful situation but it seems probable that the same individual may over-react to stress in one situation but not in another.

Despite some contradictory evidence, it seems fairly clear that the personality dimensions of extraversion and neuroticism are related to differences in learning among individuals. What is less clear, however, is the extent, and the way in which learning might be influenced by personality variables. The position is a complex one and any relationship is very much dependent upon factors peculiar to each particular learning situation.

This is an appropriate stage to summarize the most important findings from laboratory research. The evidence is fairly conclusive that there is an optimum level of arousal for learning, both high and low levels being associated with a decline in performance, although for high levels of arousal this does not apply in the case of easy tasks. This means that introverts, with habitually higher levels of arousal than extraverts, could be at a disadvantage on more difficult tasks by becoming over-aroused. Extraverts, on the other hand, could be at a disadvantage in unstimulating conditions producing low arousal, as in vigilance tasks. The position is a complicated one for the difficulty of a task varies among individuals according to their abilities and a decline in arousal levels in extraverts can be delayed, for example, as a result of the introduction of noise (Davies and Hockey, 1966).

With regard to neuroticism, it would appear that, since arousal levels rise more rapidly in neurotics than in stable individuals, the former are in danger of becoming over-aroused in conditions of stress. In support of this view a number of investigations have been cited which show that neurotics, compared to stable people, do relatively less well on difficult tasks undertaken in stressful, competitive situations.

Certain relationships between personality variables and learning have been reviewed. It seems clear that prediction of performance, other than in strictly controlled conditions, remains precarious because of the multiplicity of factors involved in real life situations and the complex interactions between factors. The findings from research in this section are from investigations concerned exclusively with laboratory behaviour under strictly controlled conditions as distinct from real life situations such as recur in sport. A review of the research with respect to personality and achievement in perceptual-motor skills is contained in the following section.

Personality and Motor Achievement in Adults and Children

Adults

The relationship between personality variables and achievement in motor activities is an area which has received considerable attention although, for the most part, the research has been with adults and students.

The enquiries generally have followed one of two lines. They have either attempted to compare the personalities of outstanding sportsmen with those of mediocre performers (La Place, 1954; Kroll, 1967; Cockerill, 1968) or they have studied possible personality differences between participants and non-participants in athletics (Slusher, 1966; Malumphy, 1968). Additionally a few investigations have contrasted the personalities of individuals engaged in different sports (Peterson *et al* 1967; Singer, 1969).

Dinsdale (1968), investigating the personalities of a small sample of British athletes at club, county and international level, found that the majority showed strong extravert tendencies, although his sample contained more neurotics than stable individuals as measured by the Eysenck Personality Inventory. The same investigator, in a later study in 1970, of individuals of outstanding athletic ability, found that they tended to have scores close to the norm for anxiety but to have relatively higher scores than the norm for extraversion.

Using the Cattell Sixteen Personality Questionnaire, Sinclair (1968), studied the personalities of junior, county, and international rugby football players. He too found that his group were higher on extraversion than the average population although in contrast to Dinsdale's findings Sinclair's subjects were lower on anxiety than the norm. In line with the above findings concerning the relationship between the personality dimension of extraversion and athletic ability are the results of La Place (1954). He studied the personalities of professional basketball players. His sample consisted of 49 major league players and 64 minor league players. La Place found that the major league players were more outgoing, extraverted and less sensitive than the minor league players.

Similar results were obtained by Knapp (1965) investigating the personality factors of British international lawn tennis stars (N = 46). As a group the players were generally more stable and extraverted than the normal population. However, there were some excellent players who were very introverted, and also three of the sample had high neuroticism scores.

Schendel, also in 1965, in a study of the psychological differences between athletes and non-participants in athletics (N = 334), was able to conclude that there was a positive relationship between athletic ability and extraversion. However, a weakness of this investigation was that Schendel's non-athletes were defined as such because they were not members of their college teams. The fact remains that they could be taking part in athletic events in clubs outside college. The research of Lakie (1962) again showed a positive relationship between athletic ability in students and extraversion.

In a factorial study, Kane (1969) found that extraversion was related positively to athletic ability in male students. Behrman (1967) investigated the relationship in students between personality and swimming ability. His research revealed that non-swimmers were more restrained and less impulsive than swimmers. The research also indicated differences in the mean scores of those students who learned to swim following a course of instruction and those who failed to learn; learners being more emotionally stable than non-learners.

The personalities of wrestlers of varying ability were studied by Kroll (1967). He found no significant differences in personality profiles between international wrestlers and wrestlers at college level. However, when compared to the norms, wrestlers were seen to be significantly more tough-minded, self-reliant and masculine. Again Booth (1958) studying athletes was able to conclude that the better performers were less anxious than both the moderate performers and the non-participants.

In contrast to the above findings, some investigators have found little or no significant differences in personality, between successful and unsuccessful athletes. Cockerill (1968), for example, found that the one difference between low handicap golfers and those with a medium handicap was that there was a tendency for the former to be more dominant. Again, neither Berger and Littlefield (1969) studying foot-ballers, nor Keogh (1959) looking at motor abilities, were able to find any relationship between personality traits and either participation in athletics or motor abilities.

Children

As with adults, the research with children concerning the relationship between personality and physical activities has been generally restricted to a sampling of motor performance as distinct from learning.

Merriman (1960) in America, studied the relationship of personality traits to motor ability in older boys. The motor ability tests involved vertical jumping, 'a shuttle run' and 'chinning'. Merriman reached the conclusion that superiority on these tests was associated with poise, ascendancy and self-assurance.

An investigation by Cowell and Ismail (1962) of the physical fitness and aptitude of boys between the ages of ten and twelve (N = 82) showed that the superior performers possessed greater leadership potentialities and were better adjusted socially.

Ismail *et al* (1969) with a sample of 94 boys used a series of motor tests including running, jumping and balance. The research showed that ability to jump and run was associated with extraversion, and skill in balancing with both extraversion and emotional stability. Ismail concluded that neuroticism was negatively related to motor coordination and that extraverted boys had greater motor control than introverted boys. Extraversion was also found to be related to superior performance in the work of Kane (1962), Hardman (1962), Herbert (1965) and Kerr (1978). Kane was able to conclude that the competitive skills ability of 14-year-old boys based on soccer, jumping, running and 'chinning' was positively associated with extraversion. Similar findings were made by both Hardman and Herbert for boys between the ages of twelve and fifteen and by Kerr concerning the performance of physical ball skills. However, the anxiety scores in all four investigations, were not significantly different from the norms for the general population.

Support for these findings comes from the work of Wilson (1969) in America. His research showed that extraversion was predictive of motor ability in junior and senior high school boys.

One investigation which did look at the relationship between personality and the learning of a motor skill, as distinct from tests of performance, was carried out by Whiting and Stembridge (1965). This was a large scale study, involving 1,540 eleven and twelve-year-old boys. It was an attempt to show whether a relationship existed between personality factors and learning to swim. The results indicated that at both ages extraversion was a positive factor and neuroticism a negative one in learning to swim. The investigators suggest a possible explanation for one of these findings. It is because introverts condition more easily than extraverts. Early unpleasant experiences of the water could well lead more easily to phobias in the introvert than in the extravert, and thus served to inhibit the acquisition of this skill.

The writer (Davies, 1980) studied the relationship between personality factors and the learning of the batinton service in naïve 11-year-old boys. Extraverts were found to be superior to introverts (Figure 7), but there was no discernible difference in learning between neurotic or anxious boys and those of a more stable disposition (Figure 8). It is clear from Figure 7 that the performance of extraverted boys relative to introverted boys is superior for each of the twelve practice trials. It is important to point out, however, that although the results showed extraverts to be superior, nonetheless some introverts did very well and some extraverts did very badly. Similar instances of wide ranging differences in personality within particular ability groups were reported by Knapp in 1964. It seems highly probable, in view of the uniformly low correlations for extraversion and both intellectual and physical achievement, that the same position holds true for much of the research in this field. Since precise instruments for personality measurement have not so far been devised, it is clearly not possible to say to what extent variations in achievement for a particular personality factor represent true differences in performance.

Figure 7: Learning curves for introvert and extravert groups

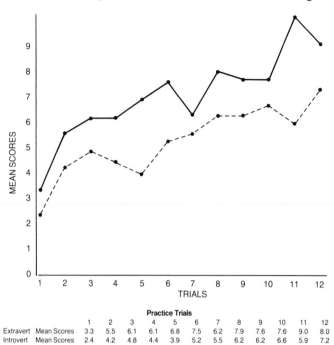

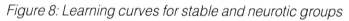

		1	2	3	4	5	6	7	8	9	10	11	12
						Practice Trials							
Extravert	Mean Scores	3.3	5.5	6.1	6.1	6.8	7.5	6.2	7.9	7.6	7.6	9.0	8.0
Introvert	Mean Scores	2.4	4.2	4.8	4.4	3.9	5.2	5.5	6.2	6.2	6.6	5.9	7.2

Figure 8: Learning curves for stable and neurotic groups

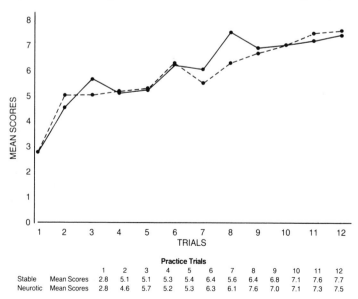

		1	2	3	4	5	6	7	8	9	10	11	12
						Practice Trials							
Stable	Mean Scores	2.8	5.1	5.1	5.3	5.4	6.4	5.6	6.4	6.8	7.1	7.6	7.7
Neurotic	Mean Scores	2.8	4.6	5.7	5.2	5.3	6.3	6.1	7.6	7.0	7.1	7.3	7.5

143

It seems possible that, because of their outgoing behaviour, the actual quantity of motor experience is greater in extraverted boys. It has been suggested that the quantity of experience is important for skill acquisition in childhood since it provides '. . . bases which accelerate the learning of similar types of motor skills' (Lawther, 1968, p.143).

Whilst not all the researches mentioned are in agreement about the nature of the association between personality and achievement the findings show a considerable degree of consistency and it is possible to see some sense in the results. Knapp, Dinsdale, Sinclair, Behrman and La Place, for example, all working with students or adults concluded that extraversion was positively related to achievement in athletic activities. In children, extraversion was found to be related to superior motor coordination and certain physical activities such as running, jumping, soccer and swimming as indicated by the work of Ismail *et al.,* Cowell and Ismail, Kane, and Whiting and Stembridge. Additionally, several of the investigations quoted, reveal that emotional stability is positively associated with motor achievement. However, some re-searchers, notably Cockerill, and Berger and Littlefield were unable to find that personality factors were related to success in physical activities. It is also apparent that occasionally there are findings which are in opposition to the general trend. Knapp, as mentioned earlier, found that some excellent tennis players were introverted although the majority of the superior players revealed extraverted tendencies.

It is almost inevitable that, in the past, researchers investigating the relationship between personality factors and achievement in sport and motor activities have come up with some conflicting evidence. This is partly the result of inadequate sampling and partly the use of a variety of instruments for the measuring of personality factors. Also it seems true to say that even the most sophisticated personality inventories are still relatively crude measures and can really only effectively distinguish between large groups of people and certainly not between a few individuals. Also, it appears that there could be differing levels of ability in samples, because in a number of the researches there is little evidence of the quality of athletic talent and particularly this is so in investigations concerning participants and non-participants in athletics. More careful selection of athletes used as representatives is required and there is clearly a need to compare groups with demonstrated differences in ability. A further obstacle to progress in this field could arise from the probability that motor learning is specific to each particular task. That is to say that it seems that there is no factor of general motor ability and, as Lawther (1958) has argued, individual differences will only be common to the learning of motor activities when these are 'substantially identical'.

It does seem to be the case that on balance sportsmen who compete at international level are extraverted and are emotionally stable. They tend to be dominant, tough-minded, self-assured, self-confident, and with a high capacity to endure the pressures of competitive sport. They are temperamentally robust. The most comprehensive survey stems from the work of Ogilvie (1972) who bases his conclusions on information collected from more than 10,000 sportspeople. Ogilvie's research indicated that the higher the level of achievement in sport the greater was the likelihood that the participants would be emotionally stable, tough-minded, self-controlled, disciplined, self-assured, and were generally relaxed people as distinct from being anxious and tense. They were self-assertive and possessed great psychological endurance.

Why stable, extraverted people tend to predominate in inter-national sport is probably associated with levels of arousal or activation of the nervous system. Arousal as has been said earlier, refers to the degree of intensity of effect or intensity of emotion. The evidence shows that extraverts have a lower level of arousal than introverts and that neurotic individuals are more easily aroused than stable people. Thus introverts in whom the level of activation is usually relatively high and neurotics who are easily aroused are likely to be particularly vulnerable to the stressful conditions which prevail in competitive sport. In contrast stable extraverts have a much greater tolerance for stress, are more robust temperamentally and are therefore better able to withstand the various pressures attendant in competitive sport. At international level the evidence concerning the relationship between personality factors and achievement is fairly substantial. The anxious introverted person because of his relatively high level of activation will be vulnerable and few people with this temperament make it to the top. If such a person is to succeed and to be able to compete effectively then his particular need will be for training in stress reduction and confidence building techniques. The stable tough-minded extravert sportsman on the other hand thrives in the competitive situation and really needs the stress of a tournament or match to produce his best.

Tennis player Jimmy Connors is perhaps a classic example of a player possessing these qualities of tough-mindedness, dominance and self-confidence with a tremendous capacity to withstand the stresses of competition. Indeed, he is in his element in the major tournaments and the 'tougher' the better. He seems to fit the description 'When the going gets tough, the tough get going'.

Research also shows that extraverts are less adversely affected by distracting stimuli such as, for example, the noise and movement of the crowd and tend to enjoy performing in the company of others rather than in seclusion. On the other hand, however, extraverts are likely to be at a disadvantage in sports in which the emphasis is on accuracy. Both Himmelweit (1946) and Eysenck (1947) concluded that the extravert did less well than the introvert on accuracy tests. For such sports as rifle-shooting and archery which call for calm, slow and deliberate preparation the quick, impulsive nature of the extravert is therefore likely to be a handicap.

Personality Research: Implications for Teaching

Implications for teaching sports skills which arise from personality research are to be found in the work of Kroll (1967). Kroll suggests that training methods could be devised to suit the needs of particular personalities. He further suggests that individuals could be channelled into activities for which they are best suited by reason of their personalities. Kroll also considers that the knowledge obtained by research could provide a means for identifying potential talent when specific personality variables are found to be related to high levels of skilled performance.

It seems evident that the personality factors of neuroticism and extraversion are factors influencing motor learning in children and that achievement is not based solely on physical and intellectual attributes. In teaching it would appear helpful to appreciate that neurotic children could be performing at a low level because they become over-anxious in stressful situations. Particularly is this likely to be the case in the learning of difficult tasks. They need assurance and the avoidance of stressful agents until a reasonable degree of competence in a skill is achieved. Highly anxious children might well be happier in activities where the emphasis is upon group cooperation rather than group or individual competition. If, as Cox (1965) has shown, neurotic children are embarrassed in the presence of an audience, they might prefer the relative obscurity of such activities as cross-country running, where they are less exposed to the critical scrutiny of others.

Introverts acquire conditioned responses more quickly than extraverts and these tend also with the introverted individual to be of a more permanent nature. It would thus seem to be particularly advisable with introverted children to try to avoid initial experiences of failure which could have both an acute and an enduring effect upon an individual's attitude towards a physical activity.

In teaching verbal activities individual differences in cognitive ability are frequently allowed for. With respect to motor skills, consideration is generally given to such physical variables as strength, height and weight. In the same way personality factors, when they are known to be involved, should be taken into account in the teaching of motor skills. The approach and content of lessons may need to vary between the stable and the neurotic, for example, as they do between the physically mature and immature.

It is quite obvious that both children and adults spend a lot of time acquiring motor skills. Additionally, considerable sums of money are spent on the provision of teachers and training facilities. There is thus a clear need to make teaching as efficient as possible. A prerequisite for this, is that individual differences, whether in respect of physical, cognitive or personality measures are taken into account.

Whether the aim in teaching is highly skilled performance or the enjoyment of motor activities at a relatively low level of competence, it would seem desirable to minimize learning failure so far as our knowledge of human behaviour enables us to do so.

Dorcus Butt (1976) in her book *The Psychology of Sport* argues that an indication of a sportsman's emotional adjustment to the game is his reaction to failure. Players who are essentially intrinsically motivated are less likely to be upset by a loss than players who are mainly dominated by external rewards, such as prize money and social prestige. Players, she considers, should ideally be participating for constructive reasons. Butt considers that players who enjoy the game and who are continually working to perfect their game can avoid dealing with a defeat as failure. Following a defeat they can become principally concerned with analyzing their own game and how it can be improved. Attention is focused on their ability, their skill and with social considerations being of secondary importance, the stresses and anxieties are correspondingly reduced. The pressures are not so great and perhaps are ignored. Enjoyment and satisfaction are the key words in all this. For players who are mainly interested in external rewards, Butt considers that these players could have problems of emotional adjustment. They may well resort to measures of ego defence where their failures may be blamed on external influences such as the crowd, court and equipment.

Examples of sportsmen who are competence orientated, who are continually striving to perfect their skills, are Jack Nicklaus and Seve Ballesteros in golf, Sebastian Coe in athletics and Stefan Edberg in tennis. In the sixties and seventies many of the players who came under the guidance of Harry Hopman clearly had a great love of the game and were not just motivated by the external rewards. Names which spring to mind in this connection are Ken Rosewall, Rod Laver and, before them, Frank Sedgeman.

On the other hand, players who participate in sport principally for external rewards could well have problems of emotional adjustment. If they are over-concerned about status, about impressing people, the stress of any match is increased and when they lose they are more likely to resort to measures of ego defence to cope with their anxieties. Thus some players use 'denial' and will say that 'It was difficult to get interested' or that they weren't really bothered. Projection is a common form of defence when players put the blame on the court, the weather, their equipment. On the other hand, for the player who is principally concerned with perfecting his/her skill, the social pressures are not so great and he/she will tend to deal with setbacks by analyzing his/her game and considering ways in which it can be improved. This is an objective, positive constructive approach and it means that the player is in a much better position actually to *learn* from experience and to develop his ability further.

Past Experience of Tournament Play

Positive attitudes and high expectations come with successful experiences of tournament play. Conversely a player who has had a poor run is likely to have lower expectations of future success than formerly and may well have begun to develop negative attitudes towards the game. Current attitudes may also be influenced by specific experiences which can have a more or less lasting effect. Players may become conditioned about their feelings towards a particular tournament or towards playing against a particular player. Therefore we hear players saying 'Oh I never get much luck there', or 'I don't like the courts', or 'That player upsets me — or annoys me'. Some players feel that they will never do well at Wimbledon or the French Open, for example, and in the past a number of world class players who liked a fast playing surface carefully avoided playing in Rome and Paris.

Availability of Psychological Support/Counselling

Particularly at junior level players who have the support of an understanding, knowledgeable coach find this of considerable help in preparing themselves mentally and emotionally for matches. The coach who can nurture a player's enjoyment of the game is invaluable for a young player experiencing the stresses and frustration of the junior tournament circuit. A coach possessing empathy, who is constructive and can foster self-esteem, who can encourage a player to have pride in his/her achievements will help a player to maintain a positive approach towards tournament play. What is required is an objective analysis of performance and the ability to interpret unsuccessful outcomes in a positive way.

The ultimate concern of the coach and the sports psychologist is to see that a player performs as well as he/she possibly can and in effect does justice to his/her ability. When an over-anxious and tense player is clearly not doing this and, in common parlance, is beating him/herself, two broad strategies can be followed. Arousal levels must be lowered, the player being needed to be 'psyched down'. Firstly arousal levels can be lowered by reducing or eliminating the sources of stress and secondly by developing confidence — some of the ways in which this can be done are outlined in the next chapter.

Young people, of course, should not be engaging in competitive play until they are mature enough in an emotional sense to withstand the frustrations, the 'ups and downs' which are an almost inevitable feature of tournament participation. Competing before people are emotionally 'ready' is likely to be counterproductive in several respects, not least with respect to intrinsic motivation and a player's enjoyment of the game.

Social Pressures

Social pressures come in the form of expectations from coaches, selectors and parents. Just as in golf there is the 'Gold Father', so in tennis there is the 'Tennis Mother'. Social pressures can serve to enhance performance, leave it unaffected or result in a deterioration in performance. Parents who are overambitious, who are principally concerned with their children winning tournaments, being included in teams and squads rather than being mainly concerned with how their skills develop and their enjoyment of the game, can lead to players becoming overanxious and over-aroused to the detriment of performance.

Persistence

Determination or persistence is almost a universal quality among top class players. The capacity to persevere, to keep on trying right to the end of the match is a prerequisite for anyone who aspires to becoming a world class player. The tenacious qualities of Ted Shroeder, Ricardo Gonzales and Jimmy Connors of the United States and Lew Hoad, Ken Rosewall and Rod Laver of Australia were among some of the best examples of players who have possessed this quality of persistence to an exceptional degree. Even when they had fallen well behind in a match and appeared to be having all the 'unlucky breaks' they still continued to strive and still had to be beaten. The Gonzales versus Pasarell match in the first round at Wimbledon in 1969 is an example of perseverance which springs readily to mind but one of the most striking illustrations of persistence in tennis was a first round match at Wimbledon in 1949 when the number 1 seed Ted Shroeder played the unseeded Gardnar Mulloy, both of the United States. Shroeder lost the first two sets to Mulloy who was a very tough, confident competitor indeed and who had been around the top of the world class game for a number of years. Shroeder levelled the match at two sets all but then trailed 2-5 in the fifth set but won the next five games to win the set and the match. Throughout Wimbledon, Shroeder was invariably behind in most of his matches but still managed eventually to emerge as champion. Quite outstanding examples of the quality of persistence were displayed during the 1987 Wimbledon championships by the tenacious play of Jimmy Connors. Connors was two sets and 1-4 down to Pernfors of Sweden yet came back from the brink of defeat to win! Persistence, it would appear, is a product of temperament and of the satisfaction and enjoyment which is gained from highly skilled performance under intensely competitive conditions.

The quality of persistence is also indicated by the extent to which people engage in practice. Both Rod Laver and Ken Rosewall were notable for the fact that they were often to be seen out practising on the Wimbledon courts in the evening and yet they had been engaged in long, tough matches earlier in the day. People who lack persistence on the other hand tend to find practice sessions something of a bore and indeed unnecessary. In matches they typically soon give up in the face of difficulty. This vitally important quality of persistence can be developed. It can be developed by enhancing intrinsic motivation and enjoyment in the game. The perceptive coach will also be quick to recognize and to appreciate any indications of extra effort during practice. It is important for people lacking in persistence to have a well established daily practice routine containing plenty of variety, interest and incentive. In this way the chances of boredom are minimized. The importance of practice needs to be emphasized and it can be pointed out that all the top players spend a great amount of time in practice. Genius, as somebody once said, is hard work.

Notes

1   A slogan which appears in some changing rooms at sports centres in the USA announces 'Defeat is worse than death. You have to live with defeat'!
2   An obvious example of this happening was at Bournemouth in 1983 during the British Hard Court championships. John Feaver made an incredibly simple error at match point and injured himself in the process.

Chapter 8

Achieving Peak Performance in Sport: Generating Confidence and Developing Concentration

Introduction

This chapter examines the factors which contribute towards confidence, or lack of it, among sportspeople. Guidelines, strategies and techniques for developing justifiable confidence levels and sustained concentration are set out.

In conditions of extreme stress, the psychological factors of confidence and concentration are of crucial importance for peak performance. These psychological factors are important in sport and can make the difference between winning and losing. It is also evident that the greater the stress, the greater the need to achieve the more important do these psychological factors become. For those trying to make their way in tennis, for example, there is no doubt that the philosophy pervading the tennis tournament scene is that 'Winning isn't everything — it's the only thing'. Thus in this context the psychological pressures are immense. At the qualifying events of the major championship events tennis offers one of the most extreme forms of competition in contemporary society. The qualifying event for Wimbledon is more a test of temperamental robustness than of skill. It is a great leveller and most players see competing in the event as a more intimidating prospect than the championships themselves. In these circumstances only wins count. Wins equate with success and losses with failure. It is at this level, and at the major national and international junior championships, that the stresses are greatest. This is evidenced by the unusually high number of unforced errors and the negative emotional and behavioural reactions of the players.

The popular viewpoint concerning confidence is that it is one of those elusive qualities you either have or you don't. You can be confident one minute and not so the next, sometimes without really knowing the reason why. The confidence to perform well under stress is a psychological skill about which popularly little seems to be known. This point is illustrated by the following extract from an article in the *Worcester Evening News* in September 1983 which began:

> Confidence. It's one of those elusive qualities you either have — or you don't. Like quicksilver, it can be there for one set of circumstances and have slipped beyond grasp five minutes later.
>
> Clammy hands, that sinking feeling in your stomach, one eye on the proximity of the loo, is something over which we have no control, no matter how trivial the cause. You can rationalize, tell yourself not to be juvenile, and be as well prepared as you like. You'll still find your mouth going dry, your heart beating so hard you think everyone can hear it and your voice taking on that rather breathless quality which denotes pure, barely controlled terror.

The above extract, from an article concerned with the stresses attendant when giving public speeches, probably decribes some fairly commonly held views about the nature of anxiety, and confidence or the lack of it. People, it is felt, can be more or less confident in situations sometimes without really knowing the reason why. There is the feeling that confidence is a quality beyond voluntary control. This is not so. The ability to do justice to one's ability, to be confident, to be physically relaxed yet mentally alert in highly stressful conditions is a skill which can be acquired through appropriate practice and experience, though clearly it takes some people longer than it does others. This chapter outlines ways in which the psychological skills of confidence and concentration can be developed for the consistent achievement of peak performance.

Confidence: Definition

Confidence is in effect, a belief, a self-assurance in one's own abilities. It is essentially a feeling of having an expectation of success. Jimmy Connors is a classical example of a confident sportsman. He fits the definition exactly for according to Keith Bell (1983) in his book *Championship Thinking* Connors is convinced he is going to win every match he plays.

The important consideration here is that the expectancy of success or the level of aspiration is very closely related to the actual level of success. Thus it is invariably the case that if people are confident and expect to do well, then they do. Conversely where people have little confidence and expect to do badly, then this expectation also is frequently confirmed. This is the phenomenon of the self-fulfilling prophecy which shows quite conclusively that in performance situations, people tend to confirm their own beliefs and in fact to 'live up' to their expectations.

Confidence: Variations Within and Among Competitors

Most sportspeople can really be placed on some kind of continuum with respect to confidence. This continuum extends at the one end to include players who have hardly any confidence in themselves. Then in the middle of the continuum are the majority of players who are more or less confident, then at the other extreme end are a relatively small group of players who are extremely confident. But a player's position is likely to be frequently changing on this continuum as a result of his/her tournament and match experiences. A few good wins and confidence is likely to rise and conversely some losses probably result in a temporary loss of confidence. Most full-time players probably fluctuate within a very narrow band on this continuum. In a few cases players with a long extended run of success, like Borg, for example, are likely to feel confident and to have a high expectation of success.

On the other hand John Lloyd for a few years, for example, had clearly lost confidence in his ability to win matches and his self-doubt and lack of any conviction were obvious to all who watched him play. Similarly John McEnroe is not playing with anything like the assurance and conviction that was the feature of his game before his temporary retirement.

The situation is complicated by the fact that in the absence of psychological training and preparation a player's level of confidence will almost certainly be changing in any 'tight' and important match as crucial points are either won or lost. Just how tenuous a player's hold on his confidence can be is indicated by the remark of the BBC commentator during the 1987 Wimbledon men's final match. Following a forehand winner by Lendl, it was said that that should do something to help his confidence!

Confidence: Predisposing Factors

Personality

Confidence is related to anxiety and also to tolerance for stress. This means that personality factors are involved. Because of the particular constitutions of their nervous systems stable, extraverted people have a greater capacity for coping with stress than anxious introverted people. This is because of differences in the level of arousal or activation of the respective nervous systems. Extraverts have lower levels of activation than do introverts and in the anxious, neurotic individual the level of activation rises much more sharply than it does in the stable person in conditions of stress such as a competitive match. Extensive research findings show quite clearly that people with high levels of arousal can be doing better in non-stress or practice situations than people with low levels of arousal but the position is actually reversed when competition is introduced in some form either by playing for rewards or for places in squads or teams or for any incentive (see Figure 9). So, this is a clear indication that psychological factors are important in the sports situation. This is because the introduction of stress in the form of competition enhances the performance of some people but detracts from the performance of others. This switch in performance, therefore, is entirely due to personality differences and the individual differences in the capacity to cope with stress. When something is at stake in sport anxious people tend to do worse and people of stable and robust temperament tend to do better, particularly if they are also extraverted. What happens is that in a stressful, competitive situation the anxious person tends to become over-aroused, too tense, too worried in fact to do well. On the other hand stable, extraverted people tend to find practice sessions somewhat boring and need the stress of a competitive situation to become really interested.

Research in fact shows that there is a preponderance of stable, extraverted people at the top of international sport. It seems very likely that this situation arises because of the fact that stable, extraverted people have a much greater tolerance for stress and are more robust temperamentally than anxious introverted people. They are therefore much better able to withstand the various pressures which are an inherent feature of competition at international level. The pressures are immense and more so for players playing individual sports such as tennis than for players who are members of teams where responsibilities and the blame for defeat can be shared. The evidence concerning personality factors and sports performance is quite substantial. The anxious introverted person, because of his relatively high level of activation, will be vulnerable and few people with this temperament make it to the top. If such a person is to succeed and to be able to compete effectively in the competitive situation then his particular need will be for training in stress reduction and confidence building techniques.

Figure 9: Performance of anxious and stable subjects during practice and during competition

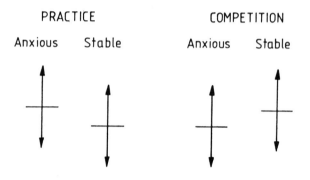

Coaching Effectiveness

The confidence of young sportsmen is strongly influenced by the coach and other people closely concerned with his training such as managers and selectors. The coach's expectation of a players' potential ability can be a very powerful factor concerning performance in competition. Rosenthal and Jacobson (1968) have shown that our whole expectations and beliefs are strongly influenced by the expectations and beliefs held by 'significant others'. 'Significant others' are those people, such as the coach and teacher, who are perceived by the sportsperson as being important by virtue of their status and ability. The influence of the 'significant others', for example, is in fact so strong that the young sportsperson will generally fulfil their expectations. The tendency will be for the sportsperson to do well if the expectations of his/her coach are high and optimistic. Where these expectations are low and pessimistic, the tendency will be to do badly. The expectations and beliefs of a coach who is held in high regard tend to be accepted and, in time, to become internalized with people starting to act to confirm those expectations and beliefs in practice.

For example, if the young sportsperson considers that the coach does not feel he/she is a good competitor, there will be a strong tendency to fulfil this prophecy with the young sportsperson coming to believe that he/she has in fact a poor match temperament leading inevitably to a lowering of his/her confidence. Similarly, the expectations of parents can have a strong influence on the attitudes of the young sportsperson if they are perceived as being knowledgeable and experienced in the particular sport.

Coaching effectiveness and particularly relationships between the coach and the young athlete is an area which has received much attention from researchers. What is clear from the evidence is that the expectations of the coach influence his/her attitude and approach perhaps unknowingly towards the young sportsperson which subsequently influences his/her performance in competitive sport. Research has shown, for example, that even in cases where people initially were of equal ability their subsequent performance varied according to the teachers' expectations (*ibid*). Expectations can be conveyed verbally or even non-verbally and give the young sportsperson cues concerning what is expected of him. Thus, the way in which the coach interacts with the young sportsperson and his/her general attitude towards him/her is one important factor concerning future performance. Thus a negative approach which is unduly critical and which is deprecative, leads to a lowering of prestige, self-esteem and therefore confidence. This in turn can lead in competitive situations to both inward and outward expressions of anger — that is to say the player becomes angry with him/herself and angry with other people. In this emotional state concentration deteriorates with the player being distracted from his task by his anger. Energy is dissipated in a situation in which all a player's psychic and physical energy should be concentrated upon the game in hand.

People with low self-esteem have a low opinion of themselves and of their abilities. This critical approach to training and the continual urging of players in sport to try harder, to show more determination builds players up to a point of hysteria almost. Adverse criticism is harmful and certainly will not do anything for a player's confidence. This 'survival of the fittest' approach is regrettably the traditional approach which is the rule in many sports.

Thus in general an optimistic positive approach by the coach leads to greater motivation and higher expectations in young sports competitors. In encouraging the young player to have belief in his ability the coach has a crucial role to play. The optimistic, positive, concerned coach communicates a genuine interest and a desire to help. Feelings of personal accomplishment are enhanced thus leading in turn to greater expectations of success and confidence.

Performance in Competition

In general success in competitive events leads to an increase in the level of aspiration or expectancy of success and failure to a decrease. Thus it is important to see that young competitors have plenty of successful competitive experiences. Continual failure not only leads to increasing anxiety but brings other factors into the problem. The person's self-esteem or prestige is called into question resulting in a serious loss of confidence in himself. Individuals vary in their reaction to failure, but it is likely that the greater a person's need to succeed the more seriously will failure be taken. Failure is depressing for most and is accompanied by the tendency to form negative concepts. People begin to feel that they are of low calibre and they become apprehensive and uncertain concerning their ability.

The vulnerability of some people to the negative effects of exposure to failure situations was demonstrated by Ross *et al* (1975) in a study which looked at the effects on self-esteem of favourable and unfavourable performance reports. Two groups of people were involved. Following completion of the task, one group was told that they had done well; the other, that they had done badly. In actual fact, the performances had not been scored and the subjects therefore had been given quite false information At a later stage, the subjects were informed of this fact. The effect of this experience was that the 'failure' group gave markedly lower estimates not only of their current ability but also of their expectations concerning future performance than did the 'successful' group. This research shows just how an individual's expectations of success or confidence can be influenced by failure experiences even when these are later known to have been false.

The particular competition programme to be devised should be closely geared to the needs of each individual young sportsperson. Progress must be carefully monitored. Post-competition analyses must be made by the coach. Monitoring of progress is important because competition programmes may subsequently need to be modified if they are clearly not working. As we said earlier, competition programmes should be devised, which will bring a lot of success. However, for some more experienced people, successes may need to be interspersed with the odd failure. There are dangers with long periods of continued success which can lead to disinterest and complacency and programmes need to be set containing goals which present a challenge but at the same time provide considerable success. Confidence increases with success and tends to become more generalized with the individual feeling increasingly confident in a variety of situations.

Lack of Confidence: Characteristics

Lack of confidence is frequently accompanied by over-anxiety and high activation. Predictably both these states result in poor performance. At high anxiety levels reactions are slow and anticipation poor. The play becomes rigid, stereotyped and predictable. It becomes inflexible and there is a failure to notice and respond effectively to the successful strategies of the opposition. Weaknesses are not perceived nor are they exploited. What happens is that the player is hesitant, indecisive and becomes trapped in his own negative, internally focused thoughts concerning the social consequences of failure in terms of loss of status and prestige. In tennis in the language of the game he/she 'chokes' and this is reflected in the increasing number of feeble returns and unforced errors. His/her general approach is negative as he/she becomes principally concerned with avoiding failure rather than positively engaged in thinking how to win. At high levels of activation the player is too keen, agitated and excited. There is a loss of concentration and therefore of control. Judgment is impaired and there is a deterioration in functioning intelligence, reflected in court strategies which are at times naïve beyond belief. Tempers are lost and in tennis penalties have had to be introduced to restrict abusive conduct. Abusive conduct serves no useful purpose and leads to a further fall in concentration.

Confidence: Characteristics

Confidence is characterized by a high expectancy of success. There is a generally positive approach to the event with the competitor thinking about how he/she can win rather than how he/she can avoid losing. With feelings of confidence an individual's concentration is good with attention focused on the task in hand. Reactions are therefore quick accurate and decisive. A further important feature of confidence is that of persistence. With high expectations of success the competitor continues to persist despite initial problems and difficulties. In contrast to emotional feelings which accompany lack of confidence, the confident competitor experiences feelings of satisfaction and enjoyment.

Generating Confidence

Confidence can be generated. Well-planned preparation will enable the competitor to do justice to his/her ability and commitment and to perform consistently at his/her peak or to use the American jargon 'to come good on the day'. The particular strategies and techniques for achieving this aim are outlined later in this section. They enable the competitor to *learn* to become a confident competitor.

Strategies and Techniques

Relaxation

Competitors should learn to relax to the extent that relaxation becomes the dominant response in stressful competitive situations. Relaxation facilitates physical performance enabling the competitor to feel loose and relaxed, as loose as ashes as one American author once put it, yet at the same time mentally alert. The programme contained in chapter 4 initially takes about twenty minutes. After twelve weeks the programe can be speeded up considerably and the time reduced to around five minutes. With extensive practice, athletes can relax within seconds. The aim of acquiring the skill of relaxation is that it should become the dominant response in stressful competitive situations such as match winning putts in golf and match saving services in tennis.

Preparation

Thorough preparation is essential. In sport this means extensive practice in acquiring the skill of the activity. Players must practise and practise to the extent that their strokes become automatic and over which they have complete control — as is the case with professional pianists and singers over their skills. They reach the stage where they become virtually incapable of making a mistake. The performer must also have thoroughly prepared himself physically, mentally and emotionally. Preparation means that the competitor has thoroughly experienced in practice the conditions which will operate in the competitive situation. Just as uncertainty is the harbinger of anxiety and little confidence, so too does familiarity give rise to feelings of confidence. Thus the competitor needs to familiarize himself with the situation he is going to face. Visiting the site in advance helps people to acclimatize, for example. It is important, of course, in competitive games to learn as much about the opposition as possible in terms of both strengths and weaknesses.

Practice sessions should not be treated casually. The aim should be to strive for peak performance. Peak performance in practice means that the competitor can be reminding himself periodically of this to raise confidence.

A positive attitude towards the game is essential. Indeed the South African golfer, Gary Player, once remarked in a television interview that he owed everything to Norman Vincent Peale's book, *The Power of Positive Thinking*. Competitors should use positive statements and repeat these frequently until they are said involuntarily. Examples of such positive statements might be 'I am thoroughly prepared and this will help my confidence'; 'I enjoy tough matches'.

Positive statements serve to direct a player's mind to the game in hand and thus to improve concentration and enhance performance. The use of positive statements will encourage a player to start thinking positively and to acquire positive concepts rather than negative concepts. This means that he/she now starts to think about winning rather than losing. A positive approach can also be developed by keeping in mind experiences of successful past performances.

Mental Rehearsal

Mental rehearsal or mental practice or imagery can be a powerful means of developing confidence for competitive play. In this a player pictures him/herself playing a match in a confident style. He/she concentrates his/her mind on seeing him/herself playing the game in a relaxed, calm but purposeful and effective manner. He/she is not a spectator in the exercise but is actively involved playing the game mentally to the extent that where people are able to get particularly vivid images these can be accompanied by actual movement of the limbs involved in the action. The term given to this technique by American sports psychologist Dr Richard Suinn is Visual Motor Behaviour Rehearsal or VMBR. VMBR has been used extensively by American, Russian and East German sportspeople at international level. The technique has been used to improve skills, increase confidence, develop concentration and become more aggressive. There are claims that VMBR can be as effective if not more so than actual physical practice particularly for people engaged in international sports competitions at which level the so-called 'mental' aspects of performance assume increasing importance. The value of VMBR lies in the fact that the sportsperson can practise visually those aspects of his/her game requiring refinement and development whether these be physical in terms of technique or mental in terms of attitude and concentration. It can be more effective than actual practice because the player can visualize him/herself playing in a competitive context and to this extent is more realistic and therefore more valuable. Before engaging in Visual Motor Behaviour Rehearsal Dr Suinn argues that sportspeople should be as relaxed as possible and if necessary should first undertake a series of deep muscle relaxation exercises.

So with respect to confidence a player tries for as vivid an image of him/herself as he/she can get playing in a confident, assured, dominant manner. During this mental rehearsal the player keeps positive goals in mind. He/she pictures and imagines positive outcomes such as a tennis rally ending with a winning volley or the successful 'sinking' of a 10 foot putt at the eighteenth hole.

Competitive Programme

As we have said earlier, a competitive programme should be arranged which will bring a lot of success. Successful experiences lead to an increase in the level of aspiration or expectancy of further success. Short-term, progressive, attainable goals can be set which result in a series of repetitive successes. Keeping in mind experiences of successful past performances helps to develop confidence. People should practise experiencing the feelings which went with their successes. Confidence can be developed in this way.

Modelling

Confidence can be developed when sportspeople are given the opportunity of modelling their behaviour on competent, confident competitors. The opportunity of observing someone performing under pressure in a positive confident way provides the observer with an adaptive model to copy and to use when he/she is having to perform in similar competitive conditions.

Concentration

The ability to concentrate completely on the game in hand is a critical factor for peak performance in any sport. Because the difference in the actual playing abilities of regular tournament and match players is often quite marginal, concentration becomes one of the deciding factors between winning and losing a match. Concentration is the ability to concentrate on the relevant stimuli to the total exclusion of all irrelevant stimuli. In racquet games this means concentrating on the opponent's preparatory actions as he/she begins a stroke. In this way anticipation is speeded up enabling a player to be in as good a position as he/she possibly can be to make an effective return. Concentrating totally on the opponent's actions will mean that only by carefully concealed deceptions will a player be caught unawares. In ball games, concentration, as every regular competitor knows, also means watching the ball as closely on to the racquet or bat as possible. The test of a player's ability to concentrate is determined by the extent to which he/she is able to shut out the various stimuli which are irrelevant and distracting. Bad bounces, noisy interferences, the mannerisms and behaviour of the opponent, the crowd, unlucky net cords must all be ignored. The score even, for the most part, should be forgotten enabling the player to concentrate on each point as it is played. In this way a player should be able to take set and match points in his/her stride without becoming too tensed up to play at his/her best. In this way all a player's mental energy will be concentrated on the game in hand, which is as it should be. The ability to concentrate in the match situation is a skill which has to be learned by practice. It is of little use a player just reminding himself to 'concentrate' during a match. He/she can employ cues to remind him/herself to concentrate on the game but these will stem from the extensive mental practice which has gone beforehand in which he/she has played through games, sets and matches visualizing him/herself concentrating on the rally in hand.

Professor Robert M. Niddefer has studied the question of concentration as it is related to sports performance by identifying various attentional styles. The Test of Attention and Interpersonal Style (TAIS) (Niddefer, 1976) measures a number of attentional styles and the author seeks to relate particular styles to expected differences in performance. Poor concentration it is argued, arises both from external overload and internal overload. A person with a high external overload makes mistakes because he/she is distracted by irrelevant stimuli such as the presence of spectators and he/she therefore has difficulty in narrowing his/her attention when he/she needs to. With a high internal overload concentration is lowered by the player's own internal thoughts. He/she may be worrying, for example, about the social consequences of defeat, about what people will say and generally be over-concerned about the possibility of loss of prestige and status. Some players literally become trapped by their own thoughts and feelings and their performance is inhibited thereby. Players with high overloads are slow to react through a failure to analyze the opponent's intended strategy from his movements. He fails to see what is going on in the game. It is important for players, therefore, to develop and maintain under pressure an external attentional focus for optimal concentration.

Niddefer considers that players with overload attentional styles tend to 'choke' under pressure and to be rather anxious people generally. Training in relaxation and meditation is recommended for the attentional style of the anxious player to be more effective. With respect to personality differences there is also evidence to the effect that extraverted people perform better than introverted people in the presence of distracting stimuli (Shanumugan and Santhenum, 1964; Howarth, 1969). Extraverts are less easily adversely influenced by distracting stimuli and, in fact, can do better in noisy conditions (Davies and Hockey, 1966). The fact that extraverts are less easily distracted could be attributed to their habitually low levels of arousal. The extravert, during performance, is less sensitive to external irrelevant stimuli and will tend to be ignorant or insensitive about the reactions of the people towards him/her. In common parlance the extravert is sometimes described as being 'thick skinned'. The introvert, on the other hand, with a higher level of arousal and thus more sensitive to external stimuli, might well become over-aroused or over-excited when performing in the presence of others as is frequently the case in sport.

From the foregoing discussion it becomes evident that poor concentration rises from two main sources. These sources are a negative attitude and the failure to ignore irrelevant distractions concerning the set task. This is particularly the case in highly competitive situations. People without confidence tend to worry a great deal during competition. They worry about past failures, about letting people down and about having no luck. As we have said earlier, the competitor with little confidence experiences a variety of negative emotions which can include anger and fear. These emotions give rise almost inevitably to negative self-talk which serves to disrupt concentration.

The ability to concentrate in stressful competitive situations is a skill which can be learned by relevant, sustained practice. Cue words to remind the competitor to concentrate can be usefully employed in practice events. Various support strategies are available to develop the ability to concentrate upon the competitive event. Self-induced relaxation in combination with positive self-talk or self-coaching can be employed both before and during competition. These techniques lead to increased confidence and concentration since they eliminate or at any rate reduce negative self-criticism and the accompanying unpleasant emotional feelings and reactions. The use of positive statements helps to direct attention towards the demands of the competitive situation.

Conclusion

This chapter does not offer magical solutions for achievement in competitive sport. The acquisition of psychological skills requires regular, extensive and sustained practice in just the same way as do technical skills in sport. The gains to be had in terms of enhanced performance can be substantial. Furthermore there is the tremendous feeling of satisfaction which comes from having increasing control over thoughts, attitudes and emotional states.

Bibliography

ARGYLE, M. (1967) *The Psychology of Interpersonal Behaviour,* London, Pelican.

BACHMAN, J.C. (1961) 'Specificity versus generality in learning and performing two large muscle motor tasks', *Res. Quart.,* 32, pp. 3–11.

BARLETT, F.C. (1947) 'The measurement of human skill', *British Medical Journal,* 1, pp. 835 and 877.

BEARD, R.M. and SINCLAIR, J.J. (1980) *Motivating Students,* London, Routledge and Kegan Paul.

BEHRMAN, R.M. (1967) 'Personality differences between non-swimmers and swimmers', *Res. Quart.,* 38, pp. 163–71.

BELL, K.F. (1983) *Championship Thinking in Sport,* Englewood Cliffs, NJ, Prentice Hall.

BERGER, R.A. and LITTLEFIELD, D.H. (1969) 'Comparison between football athletes and non-athletes on personality', *Res. Quart.,* 40, pp. 663–5.

BILODEAU, E.A. and BILODEAU, I. (1961) 'Motor skills in learning' in Farnsworth, P. (Ed) *Annual Review of Psychology,* Palo Alto, CA, Annual Reviews.

BLAKE, M.J.P. (1967) 'The relationship between circadian rhythm of body temperature and introversion-extraversion', *Nature,* 215, pp. 896–7.

BOOTH, E.G. (1958) 'Personality traits of athletes as measured by the MMPI', *Res. Quart.,* 29, pp. 127–38.

BOTTERILL, C. (1978) 'Psychology of coaching', *Coaching Review,* 1, 4 July, pp. 46-55 and in Suinn, R.M. (Ed) (1980) *Psychology in Sports,* Minneapolis, Burgess Publishing Co.

BUTT, D.S. (1976) *The Psychology of Sport,* New York, Van Nostrand Reinhold.

CASADY, M. (1974) 'The tricky business of giving rewards', *Psychology Today* 8,4,52.

CLARIDGE, G.S. and HERRINGTON, R.N. (1960) 'Sedation threshold, personality and theory of neurosis', *Journal of Ment. Sci.,* 106, pp. 1568–83.

CATTELL, R.B. (1965) *The Scientific Analysis of Personality,* Harmondsworth, Penguin Books.

COCKERILL, I.M. (1968) 'Personality and Golfing Ability', Unpublished dissertation University of Leeds Institute of Education.

COLQUHOUN, W.P. and CORCORAN, D.W.J. (1964) 'The effects of time of day and social isolation on the relationship between temperament and performance', *British Journal of Social Clinical Psychology*, 3, pp. 226–31.

CORCORAN, D.W.J. (1964) 'The relationship between introversion and salivation', *American Journal of Psychology*, 77, pp. 298–300.

COTTRELL, N.B. (1986) 'Performance in the presence of other human beings' in Simnel, E.C., Hoppe, R.A. and Milton, G.A. (Eds) *Social Facilitation and Initiative Behaviour*, Boston, MA, Allyn and Bacon.

COWELL, C.C. and ISMAIL, A.M. (1962) 'Relationships between selected social and physical factors', *Res. Quart.*, 33, 1.

COX, F.N. (1965) 'Some effects of test anxiety and presence or absence of other persons on boys' motor performance on a repetitive motor task', *Journal of Experimental Child Psychology*, 3, pp. 100–12.

CRATTY, B.J. (1973) *Psychology in Contemporary Sport*, Englewood Cliffs, NJ, Prentice Hall.

DAVIES, D. (1980) 'The potential tennis champion', *School Sport*, 5, pp. 1–21.

DAVIES, D. (1980) 'Wrong Track', *Tennis World*, 12, 7,7.

DAVIES, D. (1983a) 'Psych yourself to win', *Tennis*, 34, pp. 12–13.

DAVIES, D. (1983b) 'Caught in two minds', *Sport and Leisure*, 23,6, pp. 53–4.

DAVIES, D. (1986a) 'Examination performance and the stress factor', *Education and Training*, 28,6, p. 192.

DAVIES, D. (1986b) *Maximizing Examination Performance*, London, Kogan Page.

DAVIES, D. (1987) *Maximizing Examination Performance*, Audio Programme, Malvern, Performance Programmes.

DAVIES, D. and RICHARDS, J. (1981) 'Psychological and social psychological factors in the training of potential tennis champions', *Medisport*, 3,4, pp. 110–15.

DAVIES, M.H. *et al* (1963) 'Sedation threshold, autonomic lability and the excitation-inhibition theory of personality. The blood pressure response to an adrenalin antagonist as a measure of autonomic lability', *British Journal of Psychology*, 109, pp. 558–67.

DAVIES, D.R. and HOCKEY, G.R.T. (1966) 'The effects of noise and doubling the signal frequency on individual differences in visual vigilance performance', *British Journal of Psychology*, 57, pp. 381–90.

DENNY, J.P. (1966) 'Effects of anxiety and intelligence on concept formation', *Journal of Experimental Psychology*, 72, 4, pp. 596–602.

DINSDALE, A. (1968) 'Two personality dimensions of a small sample of British athletes', *Bulletin of the British Psychology Society*, 21, pp. 171–2.

DINSDALE, A.G. (1970) 'An investigation into the personality profiles of a group of physical education students', *British Journal of Physical Education*, 1, pp. 18–20.

ELWELL, J.L. and GRINDLEY, G.C. (1938) 'Effects of knowledge of results on learning and performance', *British Journal of Psychology*, 29, pp. 39–54.

EYSENCK, H.J. (1947) *Dimensions of Personality*, London, Routledge and Kegan Paul.

EYSENCK, H.J. and RACHMAN, S. (1965) *The Causes and Cures of Neurosis*, London, Routledge and Kegan Paul.

EYSENCK, H.J. and EYSENCK, S.B.G. (1969) *Personality Structure and Measurement*, London, Routledge and Kegan Paul.

EYSENCK, S.B.G. and EYSENCK, H.J. (1967) 'Salivary response to lemon juice as a measure of introversion', *Percept. Mot. Skills*, 24, pp. 1047–53.

FARLEY, F.H. (1967) 'On the independence of extraversion and neuroticism', *Journal of Clinical Psychology*, 23, pp. 154–6.

FENZ, W.D. and EPSTEIN, S. (1969) 'Stress in the air', *Psychology Today*, 3, pp. 22–8 and 58–9.

FENZ, W.D. and JONES, G.B. (1972) 'Individual differences in physiological arousal and performance in sport parachutists', *Psychomatic Medicine*, 34, pp. 1–8.

FISKE, D.W. and MADDI, S.R. (1961) 'Functions of varied experience', *Homewood*, 1, p. 11.

FRANKS, C.M. (1957) 'Personality factors and the rate of conditioning', *Br. J. Psych*, 48, pp. 119–26.

FREUD, S. (1962) *The Complete Works of Sigmund Freud*, London, Hogarth Press.

GAA, J.P. (1971) 'The effects of individual goal setting conferences on achievement and locus of control', Paper presented at the annual meeting of the *American Educational Research Association*, New York.

GALLWEY, W.T. (1974) *The Inner Game of Tennis*, New York, Random House.

GREEN, R.G. (1983) 'Evaluation apprehension and the social facilitation/ inhibition of learning', *Motivation and Emotion*, 7, pp. 203–12.

HAAS, J. and ROBERTS, G.C. (1975) 'Effects of evaluative others upon learning and performance of a complex motor task', *Journal of Motor Behaviour*, 7, pp. 81–90.

HALL, E. and PURVIS, G. (1978) 'The relationship of trait anxiety and state anxiety to competitive bowling', in Straub, W.F. (Ed) *Sport Psychology*, New York, Mouvement Publications, pp. 250–8.

HARDMAN, K. (1962) 'An investigation into the possible relationships between athletic ability and certain personality traits in third year secondary modern schoolboys', Unpublished dissertation, University of Manchester.

HENRY, F.M. (1958) 'Specificity versus generality in learning motor skills', *Proc. Coll. Phys. Ed. Assoc.*, 61, pp. 126–8.

HERBERT, J.F. (1965) 'The influence of personality and games ability upon physical skill performed under stress', Phd Dissertation, University of Manchester.

HIMMELWEIT, H.T. (1946) 'Speed and accuracy of work as related to temperament', *British Journal of Psychology*, 36, pp. 132–44.

HOGAN, M.J. (1966) 'Influence of motivation on reactive inhibition in extraversion-introversion', *Percept. Mot. Skills*, 22, pp. 187–92.

HOLLAND, H.C. and GOMEZ, B.H. (1963) 'The effects of stimulant and depressant drugs upon figural after-effects', in Eysenck, H.J. (Ed) *Experiments With Drugs*, London, Pergamon Press.

HOWARTH, E. (1963) 'Some laboratory measures of extraversion-introversion', *Percept. Mot. Skills*, 17, pp. 55–60.

HOWARTH, E. (1969) 'Personality differences in serial learning under distraction', *Percept. Mot. Skills*, 28, pp. 379–82.

ISMAIL, A.H. *et al* (1969) 'Relationships among intellectual and non-intellectual variables', *Research Quarterly*, 40, pp. 83–91.

JACOBSON, E. (1938) *Progressive Relaxation,* Chicago, IL, University of Chicago Press.

KANE, J.E. (1966) *Readings in Physical Education,* London, The Physical Education Association.

KEOGH, J. (1959) 'Relationship of motor ability and athletic participation in certain standardized personality measures', *Research Quarterly,* 30, pp. 438–45.

KERR, J.E. (1978) 'Personality, intelligence and the performance of ball skills', *British Journal of Physical Education,* 9,6, pp. 167–8.

KNAPP, B. (1963) *Skill in Sport,* London, Routledge and Kegan Paul.

KNAPP, B. (1965) 'The personality of lawn tennis players', *Bulletin of the British Psychology Society,* 18, p. 61.

KROLL, W. (1967) 'Sixteen personality factor profiles of collegiate wrestlers', *Research Quarterly,* 38, pp. 49–57.

LAKIE, W.L. (1967) 'Relationship of galvanic skin response to task difficulty, personality traits and motivation', *Research Quarterly,* 38, pp. 58–63.

LA PLACE, J.P. (1954) 'Personality and its relationship to success in professional basketball', *Research Quarterly,* 25, pp. 313–19.

LAWTHER, J.D. (1968) *The Learning of Physical Skills,* New Jersey, Prentice Hall.

LOWE, R. (1977) 'Stress arousal and task performances of little league basketball players', Unpublished PhD thesis, University of Illinois.

MACPHERSON, S.J. *et al* (1948) 'The effects of knowledge of results on performance', *Quarterly Journal of Experiment Psychology,* 1, pp. 68–78.

MALUMPHY, T.H. (1968) 'Personality of woman athletes in inter-collegiate competition', *Research Quarterly,* 39, 610–20.

MANDLER, G. and SARASON, S.B. (1952) 'A study of anxiety and learning', *Journal of Abnormal and Social Psychology,* 47, pp. 166–73.

MARTENIUK, R.G. (1969) 'Generality and specificity of learning and performance on two similar speed tasks', *Research Quarterly,* 40, pp. 518–22.

MARTENS, R. (1974) 'Arousal and motor performance', in Wilmore, J.H. (1974) *Exercise and Sport Science Reviews,* 2, pp. 155–88.

MARTENS, R. (1977) *Sports Competition Anxiety Tests,* Illinois, Human Kinetics.

MARTENS, R. and LANDERS, D.M. (1972) 'Evaluation potential as a determinant of co-action effects', *Journal of Experimental Social Psychology,* 8, pp. 347–59.

NIDDEFER, R.M. (1976) 'Test of attentional and interpersonal style', *Journal of Personality and Social Psychology,* 34, pp. 394–404.

OGILVIE, B.C. (1968) 'Psychological consistencies within the personality of high level competitors', *Journal of American Medical Association,* 205, pp. 780–6.

OXENDINE, J.B. (1970) 'Emotional arousal and motor performance', *Quest,* 13, pp. 18–22.

PEALE, N.V. (1953) *The Power of Positive Thinking,* Tadworth, Surrey, World's Work.

PETERSON, S.L., WEBER, J.C. and TRONSDALE, W.W. (1967) 'Personality traits of women in team sports vs women in individual sports', *Research Quarterly,* 38, pp. 686–90.

ROSENTHAL, R. and JACOBSON, L. (1968) *Pygmalion in the Classroom,* New York, Holt, Rinehart and Winston.

ROSS, L., LEPPER, M.R. and HUBBARD, M. (1975) 'Perseverance in self-perception and social perception: Biased attributional processes in the debriefing paradigm', *Journal of Personality and Social Psychology,* 32, pp. 880–92.

SARASON, I.G. (1972) 'Experimental approaches to test anxiety: Attention and uses of information' in Speilberg, C.D. (Ed) *Anxiety: Current Trends in Theory and Research 2,* New York, Hemisphere/Wiles.

SCHENDEL, J. (1965) 'Psychological differences between athletes and non-participants in athletics at 3 educational levels', *Research Quarterly,* 36, pp. 52–67.

SHANUMUGAN, T.E. and SANTHENUM, M.L. (1964) 'Personality differences in serial learning when interference is presented at marginal visual level', *Journal of Indian Academic Applied Psychology,* 1, pp. 25–8.

SHIELDS, J. (1962) *Monozygotic Twins Brought Up Apart and Brought Up Together,* London, Oxford University Press.

SINCLAIR, E.D. (1968) 'Personality and rugby football', Carnegie College Physical Education, *Research Papers,* 6, pp. 23–8.

SINGER, R.N. (1969) 'Personality differences between baseball and tennis players', *Research Quarterly,* 40, pp. 582–8.

SINGER, R.N. (1975) *Motor Learning and Human Performance,* New York, Macmillan.

SKINNER, B.F. (1953) *Science and Human Behaviour,* New York, Macmillan.

SLUSHER, H.S. (1964) 'Personality and intelligence characteristics of selected high school athletes and non-athletes', *Research Quarterly,* 35, pp. 539–45.

SPINK, R.S. (1978) 'Win–loss caused attributions of high school basketball players', *Canadian Journal of Applied Sports Sciences,* 3, pp. 195–201.

STENNETT, R.G. (1957) 'The relationship of performance level to level of arousal', *Journal of Experimental Psychology,* 54, pp. 54–61.

STOTT, D.H. (1966) *Studies of Troublesome Children,* London, Tavistock.

SUINN, R.M. (Ed) (1980) *Psychology in Sports,* Minneapolis, Burgess Publishing Co.

THORNDIKE, E.L. (1927) 'The law of effect', *American Journal of Psychology,* 39, pp. 212-22.

TROWBRIDGE, M.A. and CASON, H. (1932) 'An experimental study of Thorndike's theory of learning', *Journal of General Psychology,* 7, pp. 245–60.

TRYON, G.S. (1980) 'The measurement and treatment of test anxiety', *Review of Educational Research,* 50,2, pp. 343–72.

VANEK, M. (1975) 'Psychological techniques and procedures in sport', *British Society of Sports Psychology Lecture,* 3 April, 1975.

VOGEL, M.D. (1961) 'GSR conditioning and personality factors in alcoholics and normals', *Journal of Abnormal Social Psychology,* 6, pp. 417–21.

WANKOWSKI, J.A. (1973) 'Temperament, motivation and academic achievement', *University of Birmingham Educational Survey.*

WEINER, B., FRIEZE, I., KUHLA, A., REED, L. and ROSENBAUM, R. (1971) *Perceiving the Causes of Succsss and Failure,* New York, General Learning Press.

WELFORD, A.T. (1968) *Fundamentals of Skill,* London, Methuen.

WHITING, H.T.A. and STEMBRIDGE, D.E. (1965) 'Personality and the persistent non-swimmers', *Research Quarterly,* 36, pp. 348–56.

WILSON, P.K. (1969) 'Relationship between motor achievement and selected personality factors of junior and senior high school boys', *Research Quarterly,* 40, pp. 841–4.

WOODWORTH, R.S. (1921) *Psychology,* London, Methuen.

YERKES, R.M. and DODSON, J.D. (1968) 'The relations of strength of stimulus to rapidity of habit formation', *Journal of Comparative Neurological Psychology,* 18, pp. 459–82.

ZAJONC, R.B. (1965) 'Social facilitation', *Science,* 149, pp. 269–74.

ZIEGLER, S. (1978) 'An overview of anxiety management strategies in sport', in Straub, W.F. (Ed) *Sports Psychology,* New York, Movement Publications, pp. 257–64.

Index